Hope for Grieving

PARENTS

Inspirational Stories from
OpenToHope.com

By Dr. Gloria Horsley,

Dr. Heidi Horsley,

and the Open to Hope

Contributors

OPEN *to* HOPE

www.OpenToHope.com

Published by the Open to Hope Foundation

Printed by CreateSpace, an Amazon.com company

Contents

Foreword

By Alan Pedersen

On August 15, 2001, my life was forever changed when the phone rang and a friend told me that my precious daughter, Ashley, had been killed in an automobile accident. Ashley was 18 years old, and the light of my life. Time stopped for me on that day. I lived in shock, paralyzed and heartbroken, for a long time until I reached out and found help, first with The Compassionate Friends and eventually with a wider community of people healing their broken hearts.

Slowly, and with hard work, I emerged from that darkest place a stronger person with a clear focus on helping others. Grief has been a transformational teacher. Grief taught me to live in the moment, to value each friendship and relationship, to cherish the gift I am given each day to love and to be loved. Grief taught me to honor the love I will always have for Ashley by living my life.

My healing journey has taken me to nearly 100 cities each year, sharing music and my story of grief, loss, and hope.

Today I am proud to serve as the executive director of The Compassionate Friends/USA. With nearly 700 chapters and a highly visible website and online presence, we are able to offer support and hope to nearly 750,000 grieving individuals who access one of our services each year.

Several years ago I was a guest on a radio program called "Open to Hope." The two women hosting the program eagerly asked me questions about my life as a singer and songwriter. I enjoyed the interview because it was obvious that Dr. Gloria and Dr. Heidi Horsley shared a common passion with me in reaching out to those in grief. Though I had never before met Dr. Heidi or Dr. Gloria, there was an instant connection and bond between the three of us, which has grown strong through the years. I am a huge fan of these remarkable women for the wonderful and healing work they do.

We have been involved in many healing projects together. In addition to appearing together live many times, it has been my honor to contribute to their books and their fabulous Open to Hope website, and to be a guest several times on their television program "Grief Relief." Both women are internationally recognized as experts in the field of grief and loss, and I have been very fortunate to learn a great deal from each of them.

It is hard for me to think of Dr. Gloria and Dr. Heidi without interjecting the word "hope." Everything about these women projects the essence of hope. They are not merely professionals working in the field of grief and loss, they are healers who exude deep compassion and warmth in all they say and do. Their ability to produce tremendously useful grief information across a broad spectrum of media formats has allowed them to help thousands of individuals who feel helpless and hopeless after a loss.

This book will undoubtedly add to the tremendous legacy of hope being generated by these two amazing women. Grieving the death of a child in a family is something they understand firsthand after the death of Dr. Gloria's son and Dr. Heidi's brother, Scott Horsley, in 1983. I have no doubt that the stories and information here will help you to recognize that there is hope and that you are not alone. Surviving and thriving once again after the death of a child is not an easy journey, but quality resources such as this book can help by providing comfort, support, and validation.

—**Alan Pedersen**
Executive Director
The Compassionate Friends/USA

Introduction

By Dr. Gloria Horsley
and Dr. Heidi Horsley

This book was published by the Open to Hope Foundation, which we founded in memory of our 17-year-old son and brother, Scott, who was killed in a car accident. Our mission is to help you to find hope after the loss of your son or daughter by helping to give a voice to your grief and lay the groundwork for your recovery. Our aim is to empower you by sharing comfort, tips, advice, hopes, and dreams on our Open to Hope website, where our contributors share their inspirational stories of grief, loss, and recovery from the depths of their hearts.

Over the years, we have had the privilege of giving presentations at a number of conferences for The Compassionate Friends and Bereaved Parents USA. Our award-winning television show, "Grief Relief," and our popular Internet radio program, "Grief Relief," both provide a wonderful platform for sharing hope with mothers and fathers everywhere who are healing from the loss of a precious son or daughter.

In this book, we have gathered a variety of stories from Open to Hope contributors who have walked this path before you. With a large dose of empathy, solace, and even an ounce of lightheartedness at times, they will share their experiences and advice for getting through this heart-wrenching time. They will explain how they met the challenges they faced, how they held their families together, and how they rebuilt their futures. It is our heartfelt hope that you will find yourself thinking, "Well, if they can make it, then I can as well." We know you can.

—Dr. Gloria Horsley and
Dr. Heidi Horsley
The Open to Hope Foundation

Part 1:

You Are Not Alone in Your Grief

Words to Ease Your Way

By Wendy and Rob Lindsay

Life is so fragile. All of us who have lost a child, no matter the age or circumstances, know all too well just how very fragile life can be.

When our children are born, we look forward to them growing, learning, and maturing. If we are lucky, they become someone we are very proud of (I know we certainly were). We believe they are the future and will carry on our legacy long after we are gone. Then the death of our child steals all those hopes from us and shatters our future into shards of indescribable pain.

You know it, too; you have also walked this path.

To have a child predecease us—or in our case, both our children—feels terribly against the natural order of things. The death of a child is perhaps akin to an amputation. Part of us is cut away, and the pain is very real and intense. We are forever changed. Then we must find new ways to cope with life and carry on living, although we are always conscious that part of us is missing.

Grieving is work, a long painful walk we must each take in our own way. Fortunately, we need not walk this path alone.

Support Groups: A Father's Perspective

Rob writes: When we were first devastated by the news of

the fatal crash in which our daughter and her boyfriend died at the hands of a drunk driver in far-off Arizona, Wendy and I shared one emotion—crying. But, as the grief set in, we drifted apart. I wanted to quietly soldier on, and she wanted to talk about it. I would cut her off and walk away because talking about it just made me cry, and how could I soldier on if I was crying all the time?

Eventually, Wendy heard about a couple in town who had lost their daughter and had founded a support group called COPING (Caring for Other People in Grief.) We met with them and discussed their loss and our loss. They told us how COPING offers support through group discussion and encouraged us to join a group for bereaved parents starting in a few months.

You should understand that I did not do any of this particularly willingly. It was a way for me to let Wendy do her talking thing, and others could be supportive of her. I "went along." But, in the end, I listened, too, not only to Wendy, but also to all the other parents in the group as well. We cried together, learned about grief together, and healed (somewhat) together. And when Wendy had to be away, I still went to the group meetings. I found I wanted to be there and take part.

We encouraged our son, Tim, to also go to a sibling support group within COPING, which he did.

Looking back, it's some 17 years ago now, I still feel the pain of separation and likely always will, but I've learned to live with it and in some ways welcome it as a "memory embrace."

One change in me as a result of the group was going from not wanting to look at pictures of our daughter (because it evoked such sadness) to searching out that final photo of Laura and her partner Jonathan. I then "photoshopped" it so their faces look like clouds in the sky overlooking a beautiful lake scene.

When Tim was killed five years later in a car crash, we were heartbroken. Our experience from the past helped us recover more quickly, but just the same, we were devastated. Now our fine son, the last of our children, was gone. I added Tim's face to the clouds.

I have this picture as wallpaper on my computer so I can see them any time. I can say good morning to them and good night to them—even if only in my mind.

I would encourage anyone who is bereaved, whether parent, sibling, widow or widower, to join a support group. A group of similarly bereaved individuals provides good listeners who understand what you are going through. While COPING was hugely important to Wendy and me, many churches, hospices, and others now offer support groups for the bereaved.

Gone from Our Sight but Still Connected

Wendy writes: As well as the support group Rob writes about, there has been one other major thing in our lives that has helped our wounded hearts and given us hope that our children, although gone from our sight, are okay.

We have found that staying open to synchronicities, or what we like to call "comforting coincidences," reassures us that we are still connected to our Laura and Tim. Through the years, we have had many such experiences, which we know in our hearts are much more than sheer chance. Here is one of my favorite examples.

Several years ago on Tim's birthday, I was really feeling the heartwrenching emptiness of missing him. Tears trickled down my cheeks as I drove to the cemetery to place flowers, and I said aloud, "Oh, Tim, how I wish I could find you there." Lo and behold, when I walked toward Tim's headstone, there was his best buddy, Bob, whom we had seldom seen since he gave such a touching eulogy at Tim's memorial service.

After Tim's death, Rob and I had given Tim's watch to Bob. In the portrait the stone artist created on Tim's headstone, the watch is clearly visible. Bob and I talked of the synchronicity of both being at the cemetery at exactly the same five minutes of the day, and I took a photo of Bob, the watch, and Tim's headstone.

Since it was the last frame on the film, on my way home I decided to drop off the film for processing. Coincidentally, there stood Tim's former girlfriend, picking up a photo order. We had never seen each other in that store before, nor since. I invited her home for supper, and she joined Rob and me in a birthday party for Tim where we shared happy memories. Once again, the coincidences made our Tim seem near and were like an answer to my plea.

Wendy and Rob Lindsay are professional travel writers and photographers. Their articles and columns have been published widely in newspapers and magazines worldwide. Their 24-year-old daughter, Laura, and her boyfriend were killed by a drunk driver in 1996. Five years later, their 33-year-old son, Tim, died in an auto accident. The above article contains excerpts from stories they have written for the book, *Afterglow: Signs of Continued Love*. Wendy and Rob live in Ontario. Find more at opentohope.com.

Cliff Notes
for Grieving Parents

By Sally Grablick

How is it that we are taught to love, work, marry, and procreate, but no one teaches us how grieve?

The Victorians had it down to a science. They even had a parlor in their homes where they hosted the funerals of deceased family members. That's where the term funeral "parlor" came from. People wore black for a designated length of time, and grieving families were not asked to fully socialize. The only thing expected of them was to rest and recover from their loss. As time passed, certain "social privileges" were reinstated.

After my son died of suicide, I found myself struggling for direction. I decided that the Victorian guidelines seemed worth resurrecting. I especially liked the rest and recover strategy. This was exactly what I was looking for.

I couldn't help but think that a step-by-step guide for grieving in the 21st century existed somewhere. All I can say is that if one exists, it did not cross my path. Due to the lack of availability, I decided to create my own "Mourners Guide." Even in my state of confusion, I realized that if the basic issues could be identified, they would be a whole lot easier to deal with. Due to the circumstances of my son's death, I included a few that relate specifically to suicide.

1. Tell the truth. (**Suicide specific**) Too often families will lie about the cause of an unnatural death, due to the oft-associated shame/guilt. Telling the truth about suicide leaves little room for lies or innuendo. All that is left to question is the reason why your loved one chose to take his life, and that is something no one ever really knows for sure.

2. Control the ripple effect. (**Suicide specific**) Many people will approach you and tell you that they feel guilty about something they could or should have said or done. This is something you can control by not indulging in their speculation. Thank them for their concern, but always keep sight of the facts. Don't get caught up in their need for absolution. Your number-one priority is you and your immediate family. Address the concerns within that nucleus, and stay focused on recovery.

3. Take the help offered from family and friends. You may not have the energy to clean the house, walk the dog, or cook dinner. Even the simplest tasks can often feel impossible to do. When this happens, take the help you've been offered by family and friends. After the funeral, many people hesitate to contact you because they don't want to "impose." Don't wait for them to show up. Call them and tell them what you need. They will be glad that you did, and having them to turn to will get you over the hump.

4. Take time off to grieve. After the funeral, the very thought of returning to your job may still completely overwhelm you. You may ask yourself, "How can I make it to work if I can barely make it out of bed?" Not to mention the fact that your powers of concentration may have all but abandoned you. It is important to take the time you need to get yourself together. Remember: You aren't going to be any good to anyone else until you do.

5. It's okay to grieve at your own pace, in your own way. It is a fact that we all grieve differently. We expect family to feel exactly the way we do, when we do; and when they don't, it can hurt and confuse us. Take into consideration this one simple fact: All of your actions and reactions may be different, simply because of who you are. What's important is that everyone understands that this is normal. It takes the pressure off to know that although everyone is grieving, no one is expected to approach it in exactly the same way.

6. People say stupid things. "They're in a better place" or "You have to move on" are things people are taught to say, but to the bereaved they are painful to hear. In the beginning of grief, moving on is the last thing on your mind. "I know how you feel" should never be said unless the person has experienced the type of loss at hand. As a society, we are poorly educated on grief. With this in mind, understand that people don't say these things to intentionally hurt anyone. It's just that they don't know any better.

7. The first year of mourning is one step forward, three steps back. It is a fact that the first year is the worst. Getting through all the "firsts" (first birthday, Christmas, anniversary, etc.) without your loved one is a real challenge. Everyone wants the quick cure. Unfortunately, it will require time and work to heal. For the most part, the death of a loved one isn't something you get over. Grief is a process; you will become much better at coping with loss as time marches forward.

8. Don't make any major decisions/changes in the first year. Don't worry about anything except maintaining the status quo. Usually it is best not to sell your home, get a divorce, or quit your job. Your emotions are on a rollercoaster that first year, and it is not the time to make life-altering decisions. Everyday life will be enough of a challenge for you to get through. Just do the best you can with what you have, until your life regains some form of stability again.

9. Brace yourself. Grief triggers are everywhere. You never know when or how grief will strike. There are little things called "triggers" that grief uses to knock your legs out from underneath you. These triggers can be people, places, objects, or songs—literally anything that recalls a special memory of your loved one. Triggers will create an emotional reaction that you will find difficult to subdue. Go with the flow. There is no point in worrying about something like this because it is out of your control. You just have to deal with it when it hits, and work your way through it.

10. Have a plan for the holidays and special occasions. Holidays, birthdays, anniversaries, and special events are easier to get through if you have a plan. Don't wing it or you'll end up sitting home alone, feeling miserable. Schedule the entire day and fill it with things to do, places you can go, and people you can see. Change your regular routine and give these days a new feel. If you always cook Christmas dinner, then ask another family member to do it this time, or plan to spend the holiday out of town.

No matter what you do, you will still be thinking of your loved one, but if you keep moving, you won't be dwelling on the pain. Think of a way to honor him on these occasions by doing something special, like lighting a candle, reading a poem, or saying a special prayer for him. This will help the lingering sorrow because it is a way to acknowledge his memory, and nothing feels more important to us than to know that they are being remembered.

11. When all else fails, just breathe. Sometimes the pain of loss can feel so intense you may wonder how you will ever get through it. If this happens, just remember to breathe. There are circumstances when that may be all you feel capable of doing, and that's perfectly okay. When all else fails, just keep it simple and focus on that one little word—breathe. That much you can do.

When we experience losing a loved one, we can choose to work through the pain or let it follow you forever. Don't try to make sense of your loss. Simply accept what you cannot change and trust that with time and effort, you will find a way to recreate your life.

Sally Grablick lost her son to suicide in 2002. Her road to recovery began by reading over 100 books on grief, spirituality, and the afterlife. A seeker by nature, she began formulating a recovery plan by exploring the ideas presented within these books. Knowing her efforts would benefit others, she created the "cliff notes" to grief, and she shares the lessons learned, tools used and insights gained in her book, *The Reason: Help and Hope for Those Who Grieve*. Learn more at www.opentohope.com.

Finding Spring Again after the Death of a Child

By Cathy Seehuetter

We are finally at the end of what has often been a brutal winter. While gazing at the mountains of snow piled high in my front yard and the foot-long icicles hanging from my roof, it has been hard to imagine that spring would ever come. We have endured bitter cold winds that have chilled us to the bone and treacherous roads that we have cautiously traveled. The days have been long and dark. No matter how long I have been a native of the Upper Midwest, I know we all will be glad when it comes to an end.

As I described these thoughts about winter, I felt as if I was describing the days of my early grief. At that point, I did not believe that a day would ever come when I would thaw from the chill that had overtaken my body and mind. The bleakness of my existence during those first months after Nina died is almost too frightening to remember; it is so difficult to even conceive of that much pain. I was anesthetized from some of its cruelness by the protective blanket of numbness that blessedly shielded me from the gale force of such overpowering sorrow.

How could I ever feel spring in my heart again?

Spring had always been my favorite season. The air has certain freshness to it that I would drink in. Simply put, it always made me feel happy and light of heart. Spring was our reward for surviving the freezing winter months that preceded it, and it brought a smile to my face and a bounce to my step.

However, it was in spring when my heart was irretrievably broken. It was during this exquisite season of warm, lilac-scented breezes and sun-kissed mornings when my sweet daughter Nina's life would end. I wondered if I would ever feel the same joy again. Rather than anticipate spring's arrival with gladness, I dreaded it with the knowledge that it contained the anniversary of her death.

The smell of the air and the look to the sky that I had once found exhilarating now brought me back to my darkest day. I know that anyone who has lost a loved one to death, no matter the season, understands.

Will spring come again to your life?

In the years since Nina died, has it come to mine? Looking back at my description of the winter of my early grief, I know I have come a long way from that time of desolation. I have found, especially after the first two years, that with each subsequent spring, I have rediscovered some of the pleasure I used to feel. I have learned that just because I find things to feel joyful about again, it doesn't mean I am dishonoring my daughter's memory. I now take her along with me in my mind and my heart. I try to retrieve memories of the dandelion bouquets she so carefully gathered and presented to me, the rides to the park in the Radio Flyer, our talks while sunning on the deck and, of course, shopping for spring clothes! Her favorite pastime!

I will always feel tenseness, apprehension, and sadness as May 11 draws near, but I no longer hold it against spring.

It is a slow, difficult journey, this grief pathway we travel. It is as treacherous as the roads we maneuver following a winter storm, never knowing when we would hit an icy patch on the road and be thrown into a tailspin. Yet we must travel it if we are to find any measure of peace and healing.

Please be patient with yourself as you are working hard to survive this winter in your heart. Trust that spring, though a much different one than the one we knew before our beloved child died, will come again.

Cathy Seehuetter's 15-year-old daughter, Nina Westmoreland, was killed in a drunk-driver accident in 1995. Cathy is the Minnesota Regional Coordinator and a former member of the national board of directors for The Compassionate Friends. Her articles have been published in *Chicken Soup for the Christian Family Soul,* as well as in grief magazines. She also frequently speaks at grief conferences. Cathy lives in Minnesota with her husband, and has three surviving children and four grandchildren. Visit her articles at www.opentohope.com.

We Don't Make Mistakes During the First Year

By Dr. Gloria Horsley

I was recently on a radio show when the host brightly asked me, "So, Dr. Gloria, what do you think is the biggest mistake that people make during the first year after a loss?" As a bereaved parent, I found the question to be a rather strange one. Before my son was killed in a car accident, I would have answered without question, "Making big changes during the first year."

At the time of the radio interview, my brother-in-law had just died three months earlier and my sister-in-law, to her credit, didn't listen to this sage advice. She sold her house and moved closer to her kids, and while the move was hard, she is enjoying her new home.

I really couldn't come up with a laundry list of bereavement mistakes for my host. I can think of many mistakes that family members and others make with their unthinking remarks, such as, "You are lucky you have other children" or "Only the good die young." But I couldn't find mistakes by the bereaved. Who can find fault with someone who is on the edge of insanity, but still trying to look "normal"? Mistakes require some thought processes and, during the first year, we are on autopilot, going with gut instinct.

The moment our loved one is pronounced dead, we begin the journey into a future where a piece of our life puzzle is missing, never to be found again. Looking to others and ourselves in order to again fill the gap is a normal response.

At this point, I think it would be useful to dissect the puzzle of the first year and take a look at what one might expect.

In 1983 our son, Scott, was killed in an automobile accident. For weeks after Scott's death, I found that doing even the simplest tasks, which were second nature to me, became wrenchingly painful. One of the activities that I found most painful was going to the grocery store.

The first time I went shopping, I just tossed things into the grocery cart without much thought, avoiding people whom I knew as they avoided me. Most people still don't have a clue about what to say to a bereaved mother. "The task to be done today," I told myself, "is to push cart, lift items, place in cart, and get out as soon as possible."

I was confident that, by sheer force, I could get this job done. When I got to the dairy counter, I selected eggs and milk, and then tossed in 10 cartons of banana yogurt. I trudged to the checkout counter, happy to have another task under my belt.

Several days later, I opened the refrigerator and my eyes locked on those 10 cartons of banana yogurt. I was stunned into utter silence. Tears welled up and trickled down my face as the reality hit. Scott was the only one in the family who ate banana yogurt. I quickly tossed the cartons into the garbage and made a note to cross it off my grocery list.

On my second trip, I again labored through the supermarket aisles in a fog. When I noticed a vaguely familiar face staring at me across the produce counter, I quickly turned and pushed my cart to a distant corner of the store. After collecting myself, I began shopping again. As I selected some cottage cheese in the dairy section, I looked sadly at the banana yogurt and felt a wave of grief. My eyes began to tear up. I longed to put just one or two cartons in my cart.

For weeks, whenever I opened the refrigerator, I felt an empty pit in my stomach as I looked at the second shelf, which no longer had those little containers displaying a jolly little yellow banana. I still felt a huge lump in my throat, but I didn't cry.

On my third trip to the grocery store, parking and shopping seemed to be a bit easier. I even managed to pick up a couple of strawberry yogurts, which I knew Heather, Scott's 14-year-old sister, loved. By the fourth trip, I found that food shopping had become another routine that I had again mastered as a part of my changed life. With time, I passed the dairy counter with little thought.

Now, after over two decades later, I smile just thinking about my boy and how he lived, not how he died. He was amazing—so smart, so easygoing, and so fun loving. And so strong. I remember how he used to carry four grocery bags for me at a time from the car into the house. Now I have to make four trips.

Like my experience with the banana yogurt, some of your firsts will become routine during the first year. But many others, including the first day of school, the first holidays, the first spring, the first birthday, the first death day, will undoubtedly be far more difficult to get through. Some events only happen once in a while, like a wedding or a graduation.

Facing these events and milestones takes persistence and courage, but eventually they will begin to feel more routine. By "routine," I mean that we develop new brain patterns so we don't have to think so much about a task or action that had previously been second nature to us. After a major loss, we are again like newborns. We have to learn to crawl before we can walk.

In fact, researchers have found that it takes 35 exposures to learn information in a new field of study, as we must assimilate and then accommodate the new information. Thus, the first year is a time of learning and retraining.

How then can bereaved people be expected not to make what the world calls mistakes? Those of us who have been there know that there are no mistakes during the first year—just survival.

Dr. Gloria Horsley is an internationally recognized grief expert, psychotherapist, and bereaved parent. She and her daughter, Dr. Heidi Horsley, are the cofounders of the Open to Hope Foundation and cohosts of "Grief Relief" radio and "Grief Relief" television, an award-winning series. Dr. Gloria serves on the national advisory board for The Compassionate Friends and the Elisabeth Kübler-Ross Foundation. She has authored numerous articles and written several books, including *Teen Grief Relief* with Dr. Heidi, and *The In-Law Survival Guide*. She also writes a blog for Maria Shriver and *The Huffington Post*. Find more at www.opentohope.com.

He Was More Than
the Way He Died

By Debra Reagan

My son died of a drug overdose. This is one of the most difficult sentences I have ever spoken in my life. Every time I opened my mouth to speak these words, my throat felt as though it were closing. I wanted to be truthful about his death in the hope that someone else could benefit from this tragedy. I also felt I owed it to family members to be honest with myself and with others. Oh, but the pain was so deep and heavy.

There were times when I privately wished the cause of death had been different. I imagined another cause would not have had the same level of shame and guilt attached. I wondered if perhaps I would not have felt the same level of isolation if the cause had been different.

I now believe that no matter the cause of death, the pain of losing a child is basically the same for all parents. With this in mind, I believe we each must learn to process the factors that make our loss unique.

Five years before Clint's death, we battled the challenges and struggles that come along with mental illness and drug addiction. Our lives were turned upside down by chaos and confusion. Soon after my son's death, it seemed I could only recall every argument we had ever experienced. The tapes continued to play in my head, each time focusing on a decision I now questioned.

These thoughts added to my pain. Weeks grew into months, and I continued to view myself as the worst mother on earth. I couldn't remember anything positive I had ever done. I had heard that talking and sharing were an important part of the healing process. Yet I held all these thoughts inside. I was so ashamed; how could I share these feelings with anyone?

I remember rejecting my first positive memory. Then I realized how unfair I was being with myself. From that moment forward, when a negative memory came to mind, I forced myself to recall a positive memory from our history as mother and child.

Soon I began to accept the truth: We had shared far more wonderful memories than negative ones. And most of all, even during the difficult times, we were being a typical family responding typically to a stressful situation. Slowly, I began to understand that each of us had done the best we could with what we knew and understood at the time. It was unfair to judge myself with any new information I had gathered after his death.

Eventually, I found my voice along with a level of peace. I no longer feel the same anger and guilt. I know that had Clint lived and matured, we would have worked past our struggles. Now it is up to me to work past these for both of us. I am learning that with time and healing, I can honor all my feelings. Drugs are no longer in the forefront of the memories of my precious son. My son's life was more than the way he died.

Debra Reagan's son, Clint, died in 2005 at the age of 20 of an accidental overdose and bronchial pneumonia. She is cofounder and president of Listening Hearts, a non-profit organization designed to help bereaved mothers. She lives in east Tennessee with her husband of 30 years. They have one surviving son, Blake. Read her articles at www.opentohope.com.

The Robin's Song

By Genesse Gentry

It's spring once again. Our part of the world is turning back toward the sun, trees are leafing out, and wildflowers are blooming. Robins are again singing to one another. And, I believe, also singing to those who are grieving.

Before my daughter, Lori, died, I was under the misconception that only the English robin had a glorious song. That smaller, red-breasted scalawag of a bird delights all who hear it, and I had felt that we in the United States had been shortchanged when they'd misnamed its larger, boring American cousin the same sweet name. All I'd ever heard our robins do was cheep!

Then one June day, almost a year after Lori died, during one of the darkest times of my grief, my ears and heart flew open with surprise at a song I heard outside my window. I distinctly heard, in the midst of my pain, a bird singing loudly and clearly, "Cheer up! Cheer up! Cheerio! . . . Cheer up! Cheer up! Cheerio!"

I went outside to see what marvelous bird might have been sent to sing to me. I could barely see the bird at the top of the neighbor's poplar tree, so while hoping this exotic, magical bird wouldn't fly away, I went to find our binoculars.

Rushing back, I could hear the bird from each room in the

house. After adjusting the binoculars, I was truly amazed to see one of our "boring" American robins come clearly into view! He continued singing clear as day, "Cheer up! Cheer up! Cheerio!"

I marveled at this special message and wondered if my robin was the only one who sang these words. So I looked it up in my *Audubon Society Field Guide to North American Birds* and found that my robin was not an anomaly, but that robins are considered "the true harbinger of spring, singing 'Cheer-up, cheer-up, cheerily.'"

I stood there that day filled with wonder. I wasn't hearing things. There it was in the bird book: "Cheer-up, cheer-up, cheerily." I thought to myself, Cheerily . . . No, that isn't what I hear.

We had lived in England for a year, and our family, especially Lori, who loved to put on an English accent, often said "Cheerio!" to one another when we meant "Goodbye" or "See you later!" There was no doubt in my mind as I stood there listening. It was "cheerio." Lori could have found no more perfect way to try to cheer me up and say hello!

Nine springs have passed since then, and although I will always deeply miss Lori's physical presence in my life, those darkest of times are thankfully now mostly in the past. It is spring once again, and as I hear the robin singing so hopefully in the highest branches, it takes me back to that summer day, and I smile, remembering. And I think of all those who are now in the darkest depths of their own grief and pray they too will hear this lovely song.

G enesse Gentry's daughter, Lori, died in a car accident in 1991. Genesse is the author of *Catching the Light: Coming*

Back to Life After the Death of a Child. The above article is an excerpt from that book. She is active in The Compassionate Friends, currently serving on the steering committee of The Compassionate Friends Marin, as well as regional coordinator for northern California. She presents writing workshops at national and local grief conferences. Read more at www. opentohope.com.

The Burden Basket:
Why Some Prayers Go
Unanswered

By Judy Wolf

In the children's hospital in Salt Lake City, there is a small meditation room where one can have a quiet "heart-to-heart" talk with God. Families are encouraged to release worries about their children's health by writing a note to God and placing it in a Native American "burden basket." Periodically, the chaplain burns the notes, a symbolic letting go of one's burdens, turning them over to God.

In 2001, I became a devout member of the Burden Basket society when my oldest son, Joe, then 13, was hit by a car while crossing the street to accept a ride home from church. "God, whatever it takes, please save my child," I wrote. I was not above begging, pleading, negotiating, or making outlandish promises to seal the deal.

My prayers went unanswered. Or, more precisely, I did not get the answer I desperately sought.

Joe's body survived the accident, but he never recovered any meaningful function because of severe brain injury. He "lived" for three years, requiring total care 24 hours a day, ultimately dying of pneumonia. We tried everything to restore his consciousness—surgeries, therapies, drugs, stimulation, and even some alternative approaches. Still, we had no miracle . . . just a very surreal, quiet, long goodbye to our beloved son.

In the years since his death, I have revisited the mystery of the Burden Basket many times. Why are miracles granted to some and not to others? When a child's life is saved, families gush with gratitude and, at times, a prideful certainty that their prayers were the tipping point. Joe received hundreds of prayers from dozens of different faith communities. I don't begrudge another's miracle or their exuberance, but I would give anything, literally anything, to have Joe alive today.

After his death, I struggled to make sense of our prolonged and painful loss. I wrestled with "God, why?" in prayer and meditation. I poured out my heart, uncensored. After my sobbing subsided, I learned to listen deeply.

As an interfaith minister, I sometimes companion newly bereaved parents. I journey with them as they struggle to reconcile their loss even as I continue to wrestle with mine. I've come to learn that we all find solace in different ways. Some rely on a faith with a formal plan for salvation and reunion. Others come to accept life on life's terms, relying more on a philosophy than a theology. For still others, it remains an unanswerable mystery.

The question of "why?" no longer haunts me. What if the death of a child is something that just happens, despite our best efforts? What if it's not God deciding to save this one or that one? What if life, by design, is a risky proposition? Nobody is immune from illness, injury, disease, or death, no matter how loved, no matter how heavily prayed for, no matter how young or undeserving.

Life in a physical body is fragile, sacred, and precious. It is also "real time."

Joe's short life was his gift to us. If I dwell on his death, I miss the much larger gift of his life and consequently my own. I didn't die with Joe; I am still here. I hold his heart tenderly in my heart, the sweet memory of his life never far from my thoughts. Today is my precious gift. Today I choose to honor his life by living my own.

Judy Wolf's son, Joe, was struck by a car in 2001, sustaining a severe brain injury. He never regained consciousness but survived for three more years after the accident. To stay emotionally and spiritually afloat through the crisis, Judy enrolled in an interfaith seminary. She was ordained an interfaith (nondenominational) minister and serves families who are suffering the critical illness, injury, or death of a child. Read more at www.opentohope.com.

Grieving Dad
Defines "Courage"

By Kelly Farley

Courage. It's a word that paints many different images in our minds. Each one of us has a different picture of what courage looks and feels like. This may change for us based on events we have experienced throughout our life. I want to tell you a little bit about my recent experience and how I, a bereaved dad, view courage.

I was recently a guest workshop presenter at the national conference for Bereaved Parents USA. This was my first presentation on the subject of child loss and how it impacts dads. Although I am not a professional speaker or a professional grief counselor, I believe I am an expert on the subject, because I lost two children during an 18-month period.

I admit I was a little nervous before the start of my workshop. However, all of those nervous feelings went away when I observed the dads entering the room. I knew the look on many of their faces and could see the burdens they were carrying.

Their body language said it all: Heads hanging a little low, not making much eye contact, nervous energy and sadness in their eyes, slightly hesitant about what they were about to get themselves into. However, many of them also had the look that said, "Somebody, please help me." I know that look, because I wore it before I searched for help.

Not all the dads who showed up had the look of despair; in fact, many of them showed signs of healing. They offered smiles and handshakes to the other dads who sat near them. Although the loss of a child is a wound that will never completely heal, they were finding ways to smile and laugh again without the guilt. They were showing a lot of courage by reaching out to the dads who were still stuck and stricken with grief.

All the guys who attended this workshop appeared to be searching for some sign or semblance of what they themselves were feeling and experiencing, trying to find some "normalcy" in a not-so-normal situation.

There is comfort in knowing that others are experiencing many of the same emotions and life struggles brought on by the unfortunate circumstance of losing a child. It's confirmation that you're not alone or losing your mind, that everything you're feeling is normal—even the stuff you are afraid to tell others.

I witnessed a large group of dads opening up and telling stories about their loss, their child, their pain. What I witnessed was courage.

- Courage to get out of bed that day: Some of these guys were newly bereaved (under a year), and although this may sound weird to someone who hasn't lost a child, there are many guys who don't want to get up and face another day without their son or daughter. They don't want to go out of the house and try to blend back into society.

- Courage to be at this event: To walk into a room of strangers dealing with child loss makes it hard to contain your own emotions. You know the pain the others are feeling. Seeing them is another reminder of what you yourself are dealing with. Although it's comforting to be around other bereaved parents, it still takes courage.

+ Courage to comfort another guy: To be able to reach out and put your hand on another dad's shoulder or offer him a tissue to wipe away his tears takes a lot of courage for men. Most of us become very uncomfortable when others, especially men, become emotionally distraught. What changes this is having someone reach out to you in these moments and provide compassion. Once you are the recipient of such compassion, you understand the power of a touch or someone who just listens.

+ Courage to share their story and experiences: It takes a lot of courage for a man to open up in front of a room full of other men. However, that's exactly what I witnessed from these dads at the workshop. A lot of sharing and a lot of courage.

+ Courage to show their tears and all other emotions: We all know that "big boys don't cry," right? This is what we are taught as young boys, "to be strong." One thing they forgot to tell us is this shouldn't hold true for everything. There is a time and place to be "strong;" the loss of a child is not one of those times. Thank you to the guys for having the courage to reject the notion that men always have to be strong. This is an impossible feat, especially while you are dealing with the loss of a child.

◆   Courage to search for others who are traveling on this journey: There is an old adage that says, "Misery loves company." After experiencing the loss of my second child, I knew I couldn't survive it on my own. I needed to be around others who were on this journey, because they "get it." However, I believe whoever created this adage had it wrong. It should read, "Misery needs company." There is no reason we have to go through this alone. To see these guys searching out other grieving dads is courageous. Not only are they helping others, they are also helping themselves.

I am honored by all the dads who had the courage to show up to this workshop and share their stories. Thank you to the dads who told me that what I was doing is making a difference. They inspire me to continue my work with my web-based Grieving Dads project. My main objective is to bring awareness to what dads deal with after the loss of a child and to offer some sort of healing to other grieving dads along the way.

Kelly Farley is a bereaved father who experienced the loss of his two children over an 18-month span. He lost his daughter, Katie, in 2004 and his son, Noah, in 2006. During that time he realized that there is a lack of support services available to fathers suffering such a loss. As a result, he is working on his first book as a resource for grieving dads. He also created and maintains a website for this project. Read his articles at www.opentohope.com.

The Year of Firsts

By Jean Ann Williams

Imagine a young son who has struggled his whole life with pain and illness. His parents have cared for his physical needs and felt responsible for his emotional well-being. Now, imagine they are witnessing their 25-year-old son die from a bullet by his own hand.

That profound moment began our long year of firsts. I know my husband had his own list of firsts, but mine began with disbelief the morning after his death.

Each reminder of Joshua not being there was gut-wrenching throughout that first year, but there was grace, too, which I never expected.

Until Easter, my days included crying and eating, and three hours of sleep. When Easter Sunday arrived, the last thing I wanted was to attend a family gathering. But I joined my relatives, even though I cried nonstop while the women gathered around to comfort me.

As the weeks dragged on, I became a recluse. I wanted to stay home where my son closed his eyes for eternal sleep and I felt his final heartbroken goodbye. Sometimes I wandered through the house with my Bible against my chest, for it seemed my very skin would crawl from me and I would surely die.

My husband noticed that I needed a reprieve, and he took

me out to dinner every night that first year. To ease the pain we both felt, we went on motorcycle rides through the countryside. We watched movies on our home screen to make us laugh.

As the Fourth of July approached, my terror grew until I felt I would suffocate. Loud popping sounds already made me jumpy and feel as if I would faint. How would I ever stand the noise of fireworks? So we went to a retreat-like setting for the night of the Fourth. The place had no TVs or radios and, best of all, no fireworks. We relaxed and slept better than we had in months.

That first year, any mention of birthdays made us cry. Our whole family suffered from Joshua's absence. For Joshua's own birthday, our granddaughters wanted to remember their Uncle Joshy in some special way. My husband made a wooden candleholder, and we placed a candle inside and kept it lit in celebration of Joshua's life. When our daughter and family arrived, we ate Joshua's favorite cake: New Orleans chocolate. It was a quiet and respectful time to remember his birth.

Within that first year, I found out about The Compassionate Friends International. I began getting their newsletter, and I called the chapter leader and we made plans to meet at a park. We greeted each other with a hug and sat on the lawn to talk. Half an hour into our visit, I knew I could trust her with my greatest fear. I said, "Susan, I feel like I'm going insane."

She gave me a knowing look. "I felt the same way at first, but it will pass."

That day began a new normal for me because of Susan's honesty about what I was going through.

Still, with the winter holidays looming, I wanted to sleep and not wake until spring. Joshua loved that time of year more than any other and now we'd go through the motions. To complicate matters, I caught one virus after another, and my brain stayed fuzzy and confused. To my surprise, though, I gained comfort during the holidays by being with family.

At our Thanksgiving Day table, my husband suggested that everyone say why he or she was thankful. When it came my turn, I said, "I'm glad for us being together."

To prepare for Christmas, our granddaughters and I created tree decorations and baked Uncle Joshy's favorite cookies. With my dining room covered in glitter and candy sprinkles, we made happy memories.

On the anniversary of Joshua's death, a small group of family members met at the cemetery. We placed Joshua's ashes in their resting place. I grabbed a handful of dirt and let it fall onto the urn. Even though we brought a shovel to cover the hole, I got on my knees and began pushing in the dirt. With every thud made by the dirt falling, I cried harder.

Soon, my son-in-law squatted next to me, patting my back with one hand and pushing the dirt with the other. My sister-in-law joined me on the other side, and whispered, "You are the strongest person I've ever known."

I responded, "But I feel so weak."

Never will I forget the kindness those two people showed me on another one of the hardest days of my life.

When I woke the next morning, an odd thing happened. I looked around at the thick dust that covered my furniture and shelves and gasped. I hadn't noticed the dust for a year. As I cleaned my home, a heavy burden lifted. My son's remains rested in the ground, and a beautiful stone lay at the head of his grave. One of the inscriptions we chose for Joshua's stone came from a crumpled note we found among his things: LOVE TRUTH.

Through this hard year of firsts, the feeling of horror on the day Joshua died has been replaced with God's loving presence. It has helped us focus on how grateful we are for the time we had with our son.

Jean Williams, a freelance writer, lost her young adult son, Joshua, to suicide in 2004. She lives in Southern Oregon in a mountain valley community where she works on short stories for adults and novels for young people. She grows a large garden on an acre of land with her husband, who is a retired police detective. Jean is the mother of three grown children and grandmother of 12. Read more about Jean at www.opentohope. com.

When the Heavens Go Dark

By John French

Out beyond the silence of eternal night,
within the void of voiceless echoes,
between the folds of dark and light.
In somber streams of starlight.
In the waves of ebb and flow.
Heaven exceeds eternal planes.
Though, it remains closer than we know.

There was a time when the stars were a great source of inspiration and contentment for me. Their slow, predictable progression seemed to calm some of the anxiety brought on by a chaotic world. The incomprehensible distances and incalculable numbers were a humbling reminder of my insignificance, while at the same time, the vastness and complexity made me feel as if I were a part of something great.

It recently occurred to me that over the last six months, since my son's death, I have not acknowledged a single star, and even the moon has escaped my view—which, to be honest, doesn't surprise me, considering my mood has been steadily waning.

The death of my son not only decimated my world, it enveloped every aspect of my life.

My universe imploded the moment his heart ceased to beat. So now when the galaxy does cross my mind, it only perturbs me. It no longer exacts a sense of awe, nor does it bring me any peace. It only serves to remind me that the singularity of an individual is expounded by the gravity of death. And the loss of a child is beyond the scope of any conceivable horizon.

I can only describe it as a black hole of sorrow in which every emotion is compressed and compounded in the vacuum of grief. It is an inescapable vortex that drags me down and wears me thin.

I don't think anyone would dispute that our children are the center of our emotional cosmos. My world certainly revolved around my son. When that hope is extinguished, you live in perpetual oblivion where nothing sparks your interest or distracts you from your pain.

In some strange way, it's disheartening to see that the world is persevering and that the heavens are unchanged. It's so contrary to what we are going through. Even if the stellar array were suddenly extinguished, it would not compare to what we have already experienced. In fact, it might give us some comfort, because only something of that magnitude could begin to convey to others the horror and isolation that we are enduring on a daily basis.

But despite the fact that I am overwhelmed by the bleakness of my own encroaching future, I am compelled to make an attempt to turn the darkness into something we can all reflect on.

The lack of physical interaction does not detract from the effect that our children have on our lives. In fact, it enhances them greatly. Clearly, love is still the most powerful force in the universe. It transcends death and grows exponentially with each passing moment. The tears of loss refract the full spectrum of bliss, through which we can envision all that should have been. One day, we will look beyond the darkness and see that only such an intense source of joy could have brought such pain to light.

> *My love eclipses the sun in both mass and intensity.*
> *It is not diminished in the evening,*
> *nor does it rise at dawn.*
> *It is infinitely brilliant and all encompassing.*
> *It is so boundless that it defies the limits of comprehension*
> *and exceeds all expectations.*
> *It is so great that it envelops my every thought,*
> *and surpasses means of measure.*
> *Somehow, it overwhelms the void that your absence produces,*
> *and diminishes the relevance of time.*
> *It propels me through my bleakest moments,*
> *and sets my mind adrift.*
> *Even now, when my hope is exhausted*
> *and my longing is unfathomable,*
> *your effect on my life is undeniable and astounding,*
> *awe-inspiring and incredibly influential.*
> *You are the light of my life,*
> *I will forever delight in calling you my son.*

(A tribute to Brandon French,
5/24/92–8/16/09)

John French's son, Brandon, died at the age of 17 in August of 2009 from an undiagnosed heart condition. Brandon's sudden death has inspired John to share his writing with the world, in the hope that something beneficial will stem from his mourning. John lives in Highland, Michigan, with his wife of 21 years, Michelle, and his daughter, Veronica. John's articles can be read at www.opentohope.com.

Part 2:

Pathways
to Healing

Continuing
Your Connection

By Dr. Gloria Horsley
and Dr. Heidi Horsley

Scott is dead! These are the dreaded words that no parent or sibling should ever have to hear, words that irrevocably changed our lives forever. We heard these words 28 years ago, when Scott Preston Horsley, our beloved son and brother, died in a fiery collision when he was a passenger in a car that hydroplaned and slammed into a bridge abutment. He was only 17 years old. In an instant, his life was snuffed out, and our lives were suddenly turned upside down, plunging us into the dark depths of grief.

As our journey of grief began, we looked to others further along in the grief process for guidance and strength. The journey was bumpy. Grief came in choppy, unpredictable waves. The seminal thinker Elisabeth Kübler-Ross wrote about moving through five stages (denial, anger, bargaining, depression, and acceptance) to deal with a loss. Acceptance is seen as the final stage and the goal to recovery. We certainly did recognize those feelings as we grieved for Scott.

But many well-meaning people told us we would eventually move on with our lives, get over it, and find closure. In the past, the bereaved have been told that moving on, cutting ties, and disengaging from deceased loved ones would help them get on with their lives. In fact, many mental health professionals saw this as an important part of the grief process.

These concepts were not comforting and did not make sense to us. We didn't want to "get over" Scott. To "get over" him felt somehow like we were erasing him from our lives. Scott is the only son and brother we will ever have. To deny our relationships with him would be to deny an important part of our family.

We realized that we wanted to continue having a relationship with him. In fact, research now shows that maintaining a connection with the deceased is actually adaptive and emotionally sustains people. In other words, we are now encouraged to maintain emotional bonds by incorporating the deceased into our lives, while simultaneously investing in new relationships and moving on in productive ways.

One of the projects we undertook in memory of Scott was to collaborate on a book, *Teen Grief Relief: Parenting with Understanding, Support and Guidance*. Also, as a mother-daughter team, we host a radio show and an award-winning television show called "Grief Relief," and we dedicate each show to Scott. He will always be an important part of our lives. Over the years, our connections to him have changed and evolved, but they have not lessened, nor do we want them to. Our memories bring us comfort and emotionally sustain us.

At this point you may be asking, "How do I incorporate my deceased son or daughter into my life and embrace the future without them?" It does take time and patience. If you are in the early stages of grief or under stress, we suggest you start by first taking care of your personal welfare. Find opportunities to tell your story and talk about your child. Grief groups like The Compassionate Friends provide a great forum for this. Talking about your child, sibling, or other loved one allows you to begin developing those lasting memories that will sustain you and become part of the tapestry of your life.

It is our experience that as time goes on, your journey will become less painful and you will naturally begin to recognize and cherish memories or little moments that will bring you comfort and joy. In other words, the continuing bonds will become bonds of light that will help ease the fear that you will forget your loved one.

Our guests, listeners, and friends have found many creative ways to keep the connection with their loved ones:

- Chet got an extraordinary gift from his daughter, Patti: her heart. Thanks to Patti's heart, Chet is still going strong after eleven years. He honors his daughter's name by advocating organ donation. [Read Chet's story on page 95.]

- Dan, whose son died by suicide five years ago, is a golfer. He and his son played together often. Dan now carries his son's hat and favorite club cover with him whenever he plays the game.

- Ronda's daughter loved sunflowers. It has been two years since her daughter died of a brain tumor. This year, Ronda planted sunflower seeds in little pots and gave them to her daughter's friends for graduation. Ronda also has a garden filled with sunflowers.

- Henry and Patricia's son, and Lauren and Kerri's

brother, was a firefighter who died in the September 11 World Trade Center attacks. The family has created a picture book that they distribute to honor his memory.

+ Heidi, Rebecca, and Heather, whose brother died in an automobile accident, each wear a gold heart on a chain with an engraving of their brother's name.

+ Joyce, whose daughter died by suicide ten years ago, wears her daughter's army boots every year on her birthday.

+ Cheryl and Ben, whose son was a National Guard Volunteer and died in a roadside bomb explosion in Iraq, have established a scholarship in their son's name.

+ Sandy, whose son was killed when he grabbed a high-voltage line, keeps his watch, which stopped at the time of his death, in her purse.

+ Darrell, whose daughter was shot and killed when two teens opened fire at Columbine High School, travels the world preaching and promoting a message of love and tolerance.

+ Chad, whose big brother died in a mountain-climbing accident, wears his brother's football letterman jacket on Super Bowl Sunday.

+ The Reed family releases environmentally friendly balloons every year on their deceased baby daughter's birthday.

+ Lisa and her sister loved listening to music. When her sister died of cancer, Lisa made a tape of their favorite songs. She and her best friend listen often and have a good cry as well as a laugh.

+ Karl and Sue, with the help of their hospice nurse, Eileen, created an online memorial through the Library of Life for their son, who died of thyroid cancer.

+ Mitch saved his twin sister's purse after she died in an automobile accident. He gave it to his sister's daughter on her sixteenth birthday.

As you can see, there are as many creative ideas as there are people. Many of these ideas take some effort, but something as simple as thinking about your loved one provides a connection. They will always be in your hearts, especially during life transitions such as graduations, birthdays, weddings, and births.

Harriet Schiff, author of *The Bereaved Parent*, put it well when she said, "The reality is that we don't forget, move on, and have closure, but rather we honor, remember, and incorporate our deceased children and siblings into our lives in a new way. In fact, keeping memories of your loved one alive in your mind and heart is an important part of your healing journey."

Although they are no longer living on this earth, we will always be their parents, siblings, and loved ones. Those relationships never end. Thankfully, our deceased loved ones are a continuing presence in our lives and always will be. Remember, you don't have to walk this path alone. If you've experienced a loss, there are many groups and organizations, such as The Compassionate Friends, that can help you. Some offer education and information, and some offer guidance, friendship, support, a listening ear, and a caring heart.

We wish you peace, joy, and love on your healing journey,

and may your ongoing connections with those you have loved and lost sustain you during your darkest hours.

Dr. Gloria Horsley and Dr. Heidi Horsley are a mother/daughter team of internationally recognized grief experts. They are the cofounders of the Open to Hope Foundation and cohosts of "Grief Relief" radio and "Grief Relief" television, an award-winning series. Dr. Gloria serves on the national advisory board for The Compassionate Friends and the Elisabeth Kübler-Ross Foundation. Dr. Heidi is an adjunct professor at Columbia University and serves on the national board of directors for The Compassionate Friends, and on the advisory board for TAPS, the Tragedy Assistance Program for Survivors of Military Loss, and the Elisabeth Kübler-Ross Foundation. Together Dr. Gloria and Dr. Heidi have written numerous articles and several books, including *Teen Grief Relief* and the award-winning *Real Men Do Cry*. Find more at www.opentohope.com.

Surrounded by Love,
Blinded by Pride

By Ron Villano

I couldn't care less. That's how I felt in the months and years after I lost my 17-year-old son, Michael. I felt like the life was taken out of me. I was stripped down on the outside, torn apart on the inside, and utterly vulnerable to the world.

In short, my very essence, my power to be the strong, tough, and secure man, was gone in an instant. I had no identity. I had no point of reference to reach out to, because from a very young age, men are taught to be the ever-strong and solid provider. It's that double-edged combination of nature and society telling men to just, in short, suck it up and deal with it on your own.

I'm a licensed psychotherapist, and most of my patients are not men because of this type of thinking. And for those men like me, who are faced with grieving, it seems like there's nowhere to turn. Men do not reach out and look for the help they need as often as women do. Men are also not as sensitive to each other's needs. So when they reach that breaking point, it often becomes something they feel that they need to do on their own. Their grief is a lonely grief.

The healing process, the stages of grieving, take a lot more time for most men because, quite simply, they haven't had experience working with those deep-down emotions. Women share the ups and downs of life with each other on a regular basis, so they are used to reaching out. When dealing with a man, more sensitivity is required, because men don't want to show any hurt in the first place. Relationships (e.g., marriage) go through enormous stress, so even more patience is necessary to work it through.

For women, it means a more gentle touch, because the emotions are so hard-packed and deep down. Men often shut themselves out from even the simplest enjoyments. There is a desperate unwillingness to even talk about this ultimate life-changing experience. Women endure life's challenges with each other's help. Men often suffer in silence.

Avoiding breakdown is a step-by-step process. Fathers need to allow that body armor to come off. It doesn't mean that they are weaker. In fact, there is a great strength and energy that comes from standing up and saying, "I am broken down now. But with good help and faith, I will make my life stronger than it has ever been." The flood of emotion is powerful.

Let it happen, because once these emotions are out there, you will have made room in your mind to allow for some much-needed forward momentum.

Ron Villano is a leading expert of change. As a bereaved father, he speaks from the heart. As a licensed psychotherapist, he counsels others on working through difficult times. As a nationally recognized speaker and author, Ron appears before sold-out audiences across the country. Read his articles at www.opentohope.com.

When the Floodgates of Anger Open

By Maureen Hunter

I grew up in a house of emotionless beings. There was a scarcity of extreme reactions to anything. Emotions seemed to be secreted away inside ourselves and never allowed out to "play." In the 60s, life revolved around the practicalities of living, not emotions. Teachers ruled with an iron fist. You learned by rote and punishment. You spoke only when spoken to. You never talked back. You never showed emotion. You certainly never got angry.

Imagine my surprise then with the onslaught of emotions that assailed me with the death of my son. Anger seeped out of my pores. It assaulted my very being. I remember the anger sitting in my belly like a heavy lead weight. Expressing anger was incredibly alien to me, but I knew that I had to get that emotion out of my body or it was literally going to eat me up.

I remember that night so well. A gale was blowing when my eldest son and I went up to an isolated hill in the town where we lived. We both needed to let off a bit of steam. The wind was howling around us as we started to scream and yell. Almost simultaneously, I picked up a stick and began smashing it against a boulder nearby.

I was so angry. How could this have happened? It was so unfair! I swore, ranted, and raved about the injustice of it all for a long, long time. We returned home feeling better—the lead weight had become a little less in my belly.

During the months and years following, I discovered that anger seems to be an easy companion to grief. The focus of my anger was directed mainly at the omnipotent being who had allowed this to happen. Then surprisingly I became angry with my son for leaving me. My anger would yoyo between the two for a while.

Over time by allowing expression of my anger, the intensity of it changed. I am no longer as totally enraged in the way I once was. The anger has drained away from my body, petering out to very little.

I interviewed grief expert Andrea Reed recently. One of her key messages to someone who is grieving was, "It's okay to be angry." It is. Anger is a normal human emotion and is very common in grief. It's not okay, though, to internalize your anger so that it becomes self-destructive. Nor is it okay to hurt others when you are angry.

Try using these ideas to express your anger in a healthy way.

10 Ways to Get Your Anger Out

1. Shout it out.
2. Write it out.
3. Punch it out—rocks, punching bags, pillows.
4. Exercise it out—running, kickboxing, power walking, mowing the lawn.
5. Paint your anger onto a canvas.
6. Drum it out.

7. Talk it out with someone who is supportive.
8. Chop wood.
9. Hammer nails into a board.
10. Scrub floors.

Maureen Hunter's 18-year-old son, Stuart, was critically injured in a car accident, dying five days later in a hospital. She worked for many years as a Registered Nurse in acute care settings and palliative care. Maureen has created a grief website to provide hope and comfort through her regular writings on grief, healing, resilience and spirituality. She is the creator of "Stepping through Grief: the 7 Steps Pathway." Maureen has been interviewed on the radio, and serves as a resource for others in her local grief community. She currently lives in Western Australia with her partner. Read more at www. opentohope.com.

Bereaved Father Discovers
He's Not Alone

By Patrick T. Malone

A few weeks after my son, Lance, was killed, my wife, Kathy, received some information about The Compassionate Friends. She told me it was a support group for bereaved parents and wanted to go to a meeting.

My reaction was that I didn't need a support group. All my life, I was the one person who people turned to in crisis. I was the cool head under fire. I was the fixer. I surely didn't need a support group, but Kathy was in no shape to drive, so I went with her. I went into this sharing group, and when it came time for me to talk, I cried. I could barely get out Lance's name.

I left the meeting knowing that I wouldn't put myself through this again. The next month came and Kathy was still not able to drive, so we went back to the group together. Again, I cried so hard that I could get out only the bare essentials of Lance's accident.

At this point I was convinced that I was going crazy. I have had all of these weird thoughts. I thought I was having a bad dream and would wake up and everything would be OK. I thought I was a failure as a father because I couldn't protect my children. Every kid on a motorcycle or street corner looked like

Lance but wasn't. My wife was a wreck, and I couldn't make her better. I was angry at the truck driver who killed Lance, at God for letting it happen, even at Lance for not going a little faster or a little slower and avoiding the accident. I was guilty because I bought the boys their first dirt bike and Lance's first street bike, and I let him buy the sport bike that he got killed on.

And now I'm weeping in front of strangers. Someone told me you need to go to three meetings before you decide if a support group will help.

So here I am in my third meeting. I'm in a group with another father, John Dubose, whose daughter was killed in a bus accident a year before Lance died. John starts to talk about how he thought he was going crazy in those first few months after Autumn died. He relates how he thought it was a bad dream from which he would awaken. He talks about his guilt at letting her go to Oxford in England for the summer and not being able to protect her. He talks about driving to work and seeing Autumn on the corner and actually turning around only to discover it isn't her.

It's like he's inside my head, because he's saying exactly what I'm feeling. All of a sudden I'm relaxed, and when it's my turn to talk, there are still tears, but I can talk about what I'm feeling. For the very first time I don't feel alone. I remember thinking I still may be going crazy, but at least I'm not going alone.

I believe the lesson here is to find someone with whom you feel comfortable sharing your most intimate thoughts and feelings. It may be a support group like The Compassionate Friends. It may be a grief specialist or therapist. It may be a member of the clergy or a close friend who is willing and able to help you with this burden. It could be someone you meet through the Open to Hope website.

Just knowing you are not the only person having this grief experience, and that what might seem crazy to outsiders is really your new normal, will go a long way to helping you manage your grief process.

Patrick T. Malone's 25-year-old son, Lance, died in 1995 in a motorcycle accident. Earlier, his children, Scott and Erin, died as infants. Patrick is a senior partner with The PAR Group, with more than 35 years of experience in operations, customer service, and sales management. Patrick speaks extensively on the topic of surviving loss and has served in leadership positions on the national board of The Compassionate Friends. Find his articles at www.opentohope.com.

Healing Ink:
Writing into Your Grief

By Alice J. Wisler

A weeping willow tree, one flowery journal, two pens (in case one ran out of ink), and a box of tissues stayed close beside me. In my early confusion over the loss of my son, these items never ignored my grief or told me to "get over it."

When it grew too dark to see underneath the stringy weeping willow, I carried my pen and journal inside a house that seemed too empty and wrote some more. At night I woke to grapple with turmoil, with the noises in my head, the flashbacks of the cancer ward, the cries of my son. I wrote the ugly words "why?" and "how come?" before I could sleep again.

I scribbled through myths and clichés. I unleashed resentment and longing. I addressed prayers to God.

And, surprisingly, I discovered. Some of the confusion slid away, some of the guilt abandoned me. There was nothing I could have done to save my four-year-old's life. Even my love had not been strong enough to destroy the infection that flared inside his tiny body. I was human and really not as in control as I wanted to believe. I would have to live with that.

I began to understand the new me. She was a tower of strength and compassion; she was tender and vulnerable;

realistic, with just the right touch of cynicism. She needed protection from too many plastic smiles; she could not go long without a hug or sharing a story about a blue-eyed boy with an infectious laugh.

My written words healed me, and I jumped at the opportunity to tell others. I'd found comfort and clarity. I smiled at my husband and three young children and, at last, I didn't want to run my van over the cliff. I wanted to smell the peonies and taste the salt from the ocean on my skin.

The beauty about grief writing is that no one has to read it. You don't have to worry about a teacher correcting your spelling or grammar. There's no grade, no pass or fail. No one cares if your letters are sloppy. It's written by you and for you. And, yes, it works.

- Find a secluded place to write where you can think clearly without distraction.

- Write, at first, for your eyes only. It doesn't have to be shared with anyone.

- Write to chart progress for you to read years down the road.

- Write with the feeling, "I will survive this."

- Write to identify your emotions and feelings.

- Write to help solve some of the new situations you must now face.

- Think of your journal as a friend who never judges and who can never hurt you.

- Write your spiritual struggles.

- Write to rebuild your self-esteem and your self-confidence.

Alice J. Wisler's four-year-old son, Daniel, died from cancer treatments in 1997. The above tips are excerpts from her book, *Down the Cereal Aisle: A Basket of Recipes and Rembrances.* Alice is the founder of a grief-support organization, Daniel's House Publications, and the author of four inspirational novels and two cookbooks. Her writing focus has been on how to help others in grief. She facilitates Writing the Heartache workshops across the country. Alice and her family live in Durham, North Carolina. For more of Alice's articles, visit www.opentohope. com.

Prayer Registry Builds Hope and Community

By Sheri Perl

My son, Danny, passed on July 1, 2008, from an overdose of alcohol and prescription drugs. He was 22 years old, a beautiful mountain of a kid with his whole life ahead of him, gone in an instant due to an error in judgment.

The day after he passed, while lying in bed not knowing what to do with myself, I sent out a mass email to everyone in my email address book stating briefly that Danny had passed of an overdose, and I asked everyone to please send him a prayer.

It was kind of an instinctual thing; I didn't really think much about it. In the insanity of the days to follow, I forgot all about it.

One week later, I was sitting in session with the gifted medium, Glenn Dove, who instantly brought through my father who had Dan with him. One of the first things Danny commented on was the "waves of prayer" that he felt coming to him from so many people and how much the prayers had helped to heal him. I was impressed, because I knew I'd set a prayer list into motion, but I didn't really expect the prayers to have such a powerful effect on Danny.

One year later, as we were approaching the first anniversary of Danny's passing, we wondered what to do. We didn't want to ask anyone to inconvenience themselves on our behalf, but we felt that we needed to do something. My husband, Jerry, suggested that we ask everyone to say a prayer, and I knew instantly that would be the best thing that we could do.

Emails were sent out, phone calls were made, and a prayer team was set into motion. When the dreaded first day of July came, we were surprised to discover that we felt stronger than we had imagined we would. We didn't know how to explain it, but we felt the support from the prayers.

It was at this point that I had the idea to form The Prayer Registry to open this up to all parents who had lost children. My son, Aaron, helped me to create this free website service, which is dedicated to all of the families who have lost children, whatever age that child was when he or she passed.

This site registers the anniversary day of our children's crossing. The members of this online community, the Prayer Team, have the opportunity to honor their child's legacy and connect with other bereaved parents in order to participate in worldwide group prayer for every registered loved one on the anniversary day of their passing.

To register a child for prayer, email me at theprayerregistry@gmail.com. I need only your child's full name along with the date that he or she passed to ensure that your child receives prayer every year on the anniversary day of his or her passing.

Many of our parents report feeling stronger and less agonized on their children's Prayer Dates, and our children have come through reputable mediums to express gratitude for the gift of energy that comes their way from the prayers. It is a wonderful feeling to know that there is still something that we can do to help our children and that we are doing it.

I am grateful to Open to Hope for giving me this opportunity to invite all of you to register your children for prayer and become a part of our growing Prayer Team of loving parents.

All are welcome.

Sheri Perl is a spiritual healer, interfaith minister, author and lecturer. In 2008 Sheri lost her 22-year-old son, Daniel, to a drug overdose. In his honor Sheri has formed The Prayer Registry for parents who have lost children. She is the author of *Healing from the Inside Out*, which tells of her miraculous healing experience with the late British spiritual healer Harry Edwards. Read more at www.opentohope.com.

Taking Action
to Save Others

By Candace Lightner

In 1980, I lived in a suburb of Sacramento with my three children, including my 13-year-old twins, Cari and Serena. One day, Cari and her friend Karla were on their way to a Catholic school carnival, which was right down the street from our house. Both girls were walking inside the bike lane when a car hit them from behind. Cari was thrown 125 feet and left on the road to die while the driver kept going.

Several days later, the driver's wife, who was a very Christian woman, called the police and turned her husband in. Before he killed Cari, he had just been released from jail several hours earlier from another drunk-driving crash. He had totaled his car so he was using hers, and when he came home, she noticed the car had obviously been in another wreck. She asked a friend of hers, who was a California highway patrolman, if there had been any accidents over the weekend, and he replied that a 13-year-old child had been killed by a hit-and-run driver. She told him that her husband might have been responsible.

Now, you may be wondering why he was still driving, given that he had hit someone two days earlier. Unfortunately, that's the way the laws worked in 1980. They were just not enforced.

It is hard to believe, but he was driving with a valid California driver's license even though, if I can remember, he had several prior drunk-driving arrests and convictions. Drunk driving wasn't taken seriously or treated as a crime. And that was one of the things that I set about to change, which I did. We've come a long way since then. Times have changed.

The day after Cari's funeral, I learned from a patrolman that the man who had killed my daughter had been drinking and had a rap sheet as a drunken driver. I asked, "How long will he get in prison?"

The cop kind of laughed. "Prison? Lady, you'll be lucky if he sees any jail time."

I was so angry I started Mothers Against Drunk Drivers, now Mothers Against Drunk Driving (MADD). And it worked. MADD just took off, and there was no stopping it. I was a crusader with a cause. I was angry for a long time and with good reason. Soon, I incorporated Cari's death and her life as part of my life, and it became one, so to speak—it's who I am and what I'm about.

I think the reason MADD became so successful was because I didn't know any better. People would say, "You can't do this," and I'd say, "Sure I can. Why not?" I had no concept. I was incredibly naïve. I felt the need to reach out, to save another life and not let this happen again. I wanted to save my other children.

But eventually I got burned out. I wasn't seeing my children because I was on the road seven days a week, 24 hours a day. Going to Washington to help get tougher federal legislation passed against drunk driving was a good way of dealing with my anger, but it probably was not the best way of dealing with my grief. So after five-and-a-half years with MADD, I left.

That's when I discovered that I had never fully grieved Cari's loss. I went to a wonderful therapist and realized that I had put the painful part of grieving Cari's death on hold, mainly because it was so painful. When I would run into people and I was obviously grieving, they'd say, "But it's been five-and-a-half years!" People confuse the list of Kübler-Ross's stages of dying with grieving over the death of a loved one. Everybody thinks you go through this at this time and that at that time, and that's not true. I think people need to just do what comes naturally.

I don't get angry at all anymore, but there are times even after 30 years when I still grieve and I'm still sad. In my opinion, grief comes in three stages—the beginning, the middle, and the rest of your life.

If I had to give a newly bereaved person one piece of advice it would be: Mourn. Grieve. Do what you need to do. Don't worry about whether it's normal or not, as long as you're not hurting yourself or someone else, and you can still function. Don't try to put it off. I know it's painful. Don't worry about crying in front of other people, and if you need help, ask for it.

Candace Lightner transformed a personal tragedy into a crusade against drunk driving. While walking down a quiet street, her 13-year-old daughter, Cari, was struck from behind and thrown 125 feet in the air by a driver with numerous previous drunk-driving convictions. She founded Mothers against Drunk Driving (MADD), a grassroots organization dedicated to curbing alcohol-related traffic deaths. Find out more at www.opentohope.com.

Healing a Broken Brain,
Mending a Broken Heart

By Eric Hipple

What comes to mind when you hear the word "quarterback"? Maybe you remember Joe Montana's cool or Joe Namath's swagger or Bart Starr's grit. Or maybe you think back to your high school or college days. The quarterback is always the Big Man on Campus, the guy in charge, the leader.

It's a tough job, but a glamorous one. And I loved it. The ten years that I played professional football were the best years of my life.

On the field, the buck stopped with me. I was in control—21 other big, tough men responded to what I was doing. Tens of thousands of people in the stadium, and millions more watching on television, had their eyes fixed on me. Every game was in the spotlight.

Off the field, people looked up to me. They assumed that because I was the quarterback I must be full of self-confidence; that I was completely in control, not only of the game, but also of my entire life. But that image was far out of sync with reality.

During the off-season I would just lie on the couch for days or even weeks at a time or get into moods so black that no one wanted to be around me, or I would try to relieve the pain inside with alcohol and, later, with drugs. I didn't see these problems for what they were: The warning signs of chronic depression.

My playing career ended abruptly at age 32. That's prime time for many quarterbacks, but I was done. Actually I was done in a lot of ways, which became apparent within a frighteningly short amount of time.

My first marriage ended in divorce. I went bankrupt.

I threw myself out of a moving car at 70 miles per hour in a bungled suicide attempt.

And my only son, Jeff, actually did what his father did not do. He died from suicide at age 15.

Spiraling even further downhill from there, I went from Monday Night Football to Monday night in jail, arrested and convicted of drunk driving.

It took all those shocks for me to realize that I had what I call a "broken brain." And my son had one, too. If you don't do something about it, a broken brain can become a string of broken lives.

Jeff was a happy, funny, outgoing kid. He did well in school, enjoyed sports, and seemed to enjoy life. But once he reached high school, he hit a wall. He took his mother's second divorce very hard, especially since he was really attached to his stepfather. My personal and financial problems at the time certainly didn't help.

He began having trouble sleeping and suffered a loss of appetite, energy, and pleasure. He started cutting school, and his grades dropped. He was also cutting himself with a knife, ironically, to dull the pain.

I took him to doctors who said there was no physical problem, but he and his body were trying to tell us something. I learned later that Jeff had been writing letters about his problems to a friend, saying things like "I can't take it much longer." Plainly, he was asking for help, but, unfortunately, he wasn't asking the right people.

On April 9, 2000, I kissed Jeff goodbye and went off on a business trip. It never occurred to me that it would be the last time I would see him alive.

After Jeff's death, I became the world's greatest Monday-morning quarterback. The benefit of perfect hindsight showed me that Jeff had been clinically depressed and calling out for help. But I didn't see the signs. How could I, when I couldn't see them in myself?

The rage, shame, and guilt that I felt began to overwhelm me. I pushed the pain aside with more and more alcohol—until finally, on the way home from a bar one night, I was busted for drunk driving and sent to jail.

Although I certainly don't recommend it to anyone else, my time in jail was therapeutic. My 58-day sentence included a mandatory detox program, so I got off the alcohol and medications I had been using to blot out reality.

I was able to think clearly for the first time in years. I realized that I'd been playing defense most of my life. And even with the best defense in the world, you can't win. I needed a better offense.

I soon found the right doctor, and we talked about all my symptoms and what they meant. Together we found the right combination of antidepressants. I also began Cognitive Behavioral Therapy, or CBT, so I could understand how the brain's chemistry works.

Is life perfect for me now? Hardly. But the black clouds of depression that used to envelop me have parted. The air smells sweeter. Colors seem more vivid, and everything seems brighter.

On most days, I can look at a picture or video of Jeff and remember the good times we had together. For a long time after he died, I couldn't do that. But even now, years later, his birthday and the anniversary of his death are very tough days for me. That's OK. I know what's wrong and I know how to deal with it.

And yes, I cry. Real men, I've come to learn late in life, do cry. In the first years after Jeff's passing, I cried so hard that sometimes people would give me "The Madman's Berth"—that wide walk around someone you just can't console.

Now, when I need to weep, I weep. When I need to laugh, I laugh.

It's a lot more authentic. My image and my inner self are finally at peace.

Depression remains one of the most treatable diseases in the world and also one of the most under-diagnosed. Learn the warning signs. Remember that serious depression is, in reality, a broken brain. It's not a sign of character weakness, just as a broken arm isn't a sign of character weakness.

If you have deep sadness or feelings of worthlessness and lethargy for two weeks or more, take a leap of faith and seek help.

But just as important as learning the signs of depression in yourself is learning to look for these signs in someone you love—your son, your daughter, your spouse, or your best friend. One in five teens has serious thoughts of suicide.

I know how easy it is to get caught up in the day-to-day stuff and rationalize the behavior of someone you live with every day. It's easy to convince yourself that everything is OK.

Step back. Don't miss the proverbial forest for the trees. Think, "Wait a minute, real life is happening here."

It isn't easy, as I am the first to admit. I couldn't do it when it counted. But I think one reason we have tragedy in the world is that it serves to snap us back to reality.

If my writing about depression can spare one family from going through what my family and I went through, then this will be priceless and your actions going forward will be well worth your best efforts.

Eric Hipple lost his 15-year-old son, Jeff, to a self-inflicted gunshot wound in 2000. Eric was a quarterback for the Detroit Lions from 1980–1989. He is an outreach coordinator for the University of Michigan's Depression Center and is the author of the award-winning book *Real Men Do Cry*, his inspiring story of tackling depression and surviving suicide loss. He speaks from personal experience, spreading the dual message of depression warning signs and suicide prevention. Read more at www.opentohope.com.

After a Child Dies:
How to Help a Surviving Sibling

By Dr. Howard Winokuer
and Dr. Heidi Horsley

What we have once enjoyed we can never lose.
All that we love deeply becomes a part of us.
—*Helen Keller*

The death of a child is traumatic. It often turns our lives upside down and puts everything we ever believed into question. Regardless of the way a child dies, we are never prepared to lose them. As parents, we do not expect to outlive our children, and as siblings, we just assume we will travel through life and grow old together. Not only are parents dealing with their own grief after a loss, but they worry about their surviving children and want to make sure that they are doing what's best for them.

Talking about death with adults is difficult, but talking to your children about death may be even harder. Although it may not always look like your children are grieving, it is critical to understand that they also grieve. They experience their grief differently, but nonetheless, they do grieve.

As parents, you may be asking questions such as: What will we say? What will we do? How do we best help our child after the death of his or her sibling? Where do we learn the answers to these questions? What can be said? What can be done?

First and foremost, children need to be made aware that they still live in a safe and predictable world after a sibling's death. Being reassuring and behaving in ways that communicate to your children that you are there for them and that you will be able to take care of them, even though you are grieving, is key. Further, it is very comforting for them to know that they are not alone in their grief and that as a family you will all get through this difficult time together.

Even though parents often have the best intentions in mind, what we do or say may not always be helpful and can sometimes even be harmful. It is important to be aware that children oftentimes take things very literally. When you tell a child that someone died because he was sick, your child may be afraid every time he or she gets a cold. Kids often have difficulty differentiating between being sick with a cold or the flu versus being sick from cancer or some other terminal illness.

Do not tell a child that someone just went away, because every time there is a departure, the child will perceive that as "going away." Kids will worry that when you leave to go to work or even go to the grocery store, you may never be coming back. Also, guard against saying that someone just went to sleep or that death is just like sleep. Once again, remember that kids take things literally, and they may develop sleep difficulties because of fears that if they fall asleep, they will not wake up again.

There are things that can be said and done that will help children explore their grief and express their feelings:

Allow expressions of feelings—there are a wide range of feelings associated with the grief process. Feelings aren't right or wrong, they just are. Reassuring your child that it's normal to experience feelings such as anger, sadness, or anxiety will let your child know that what he or she is going through is not unusual.

Create an open and supportive environment—provide honest answers and age-appropriate information. Some children may be more comfortable drawing, writing stories, or acting out their emotions in a play, rather than talking.

Communicate through touch—touch can often express thoughts and feelings that words cannot. For example, putting an arm around the child, sitting close to him, holding him on your lap, or even holding his hand lets him know that you are there and he is not alone.

Talk about worries and concerns—children often express a lot of worries after loss. They may begin to act younger and become clingy and whiney. Regression is a common reaction and usually doesn't last too long. Be supportive and don't criticize regressive behavior. You may need to spend extra time with your child during transitions—for example, when dropping him off at daycare. Your child may also need to sleep with a nightlight, stuffed toy, and/or favorite blanket.

Encourage your child to ask questions—don't be afraid to answer your child's questions openly and honestly in an age-appropriate way. The truth is always easier for a child to deal with rather than the often-frightening fantasy that he might create in his mind, if not given information.

Other tips that you might find very helpful include:

- Be gentle but truthful in telling your child about the death.

- Have as many pictures and reminders around your home of your surviving child as you have of your deceased child.

+ Let your surviving child know that, although you are devastated over the loss, life is still worth living, and remind her how grateful you are to have her in your life.

+ Recognize normal child reactions to grief.

+ Give your child your assurance of love and support.

+ Assure your child that nothing he did or thought caused the death.

+ Encourage your child to talk about how he feels.

+ Encourage your child to cry, but don't put too much pressure on her.

+ Cry or grieve with your child in a way that is not scary and conveys to her that although you are upset, you will still be able to care for her.

Talking to your child about death can be one of the most significant life events that you will participate in. Children are very resilient, and although a sibling loss may define your child's life, it will in no way destroy his life. Your child will forever miss his sibling, but in time he will find new ways to incorporate him or her into his life through continuing bonds. It is important to honor the grief that your child experiences and validate that grief through your care and presence. By doing this, you can make a significant difference in his life. Remember that your openness may help decrease your child's fear and that being there for your child is the most important thing that you can do.

Dr. Howard R. Winokuer is the cofounder of TO LIFE, a not-for-profit educational and counseling organization that specializes in issues dealing with grief and loss. He has worked with thousands of people suffering from grief. He has conducted workshops and seminars throughout the United States, as well as in nine foreign countries. He has written and published extensively. For more, visit www.opentohope.com.

Dr. Heidi Horsley, an internationally known grief expert and author, is the executive director of the Open to Hope Foundation, which she cofounded with her mother, Dr. Gloria Horsley. Dr. Heidi's 17-year-old brother, Scott, and cousin, Matthew, died together in a car accident, and she has experienced two miscarriages. A licensed psychologist and social worker, she cohosts "Grief Relief" radio and "Grief Relief" television, an award-winning series. She is an adjunct professor at Columbia University and serves on the national board of directors for The Compassionate Friends and on the advisory board for TAPS, the Tragedy Assistance Program for Survivors of Military Loss, and the Elisabeth Kübler-Ross Foundation. She is the author of numerous articles and coauthor of several books, including *Teen Grief Relief* and the award-winning *Real Men Do Cry*. Find more at www.opentohope.com.

Tell the Positive Story
of Your Child's Life

By Sandy Fox

I have a suggestion for all bereaved parents to call up positive memories of your child:

First, you need to find a quiet place in your home with no distractions. Sit in a comfortable chair and, with pen and paper or on your computer, jot down a few phrases of every good memory you can think of related to your child. Make the memory phrases just long enough so the memory is clear in your mind. You may end up with 25, 50, or even more than a hundred.

They can be in any order or age. You can rearrange later. Make sure they are labeled. They can be labeled by year, by events, by honors, by family gatherings, by humor, or by whatever you'd like.

At first, it may be difficult to think of many things because you are consumed by your child's death, but as time moves forward, many memories will return as your mind begins to focus once again.

Go back over these memories and select ten. For each of these ten, write as much as you can remember about the memory.

In other words, tell a story. Use these ten memories when appropriate. For instance, you can tell a few stories to friends or family members who may live out of town and were not an everyday presence in your child's life. One of the best places to talk about these memories is at family dinners or holiday events where others may reminisce as well about their children.

When you have gone through these ten memories with everyone suitable to hear them, put them aside and start on another ten. Repeat these stories to others and so on, so that you always have stories and reasons to talk about your child. You can always come back to many of them, depending on the situation.

For example, a story I remember about my daughter, Marcy, that I like to tell happened when she was in a beauty contest at age four and was finally called to the stage to be interviewed. Her personality really shined. She had the whole audience in hysterics as she demonstrated, very dramatically with stories and expressions, what it was like waiting backstage for hours.

Typically, people will be afraid to bring up your child's name for fear it will hurt you and make you sad. I think just the opposite happens for me. When someone brings up my child's name and asks a question, I am so happy to talk about her, and in turn, that shows others they do not have to be afraid that I will be upset. What makes me upset is when others ignore the fact that I even had a child!

Keep these memories in a file so you don't lose them. However, don't dwell on them or focus exclusively on them and ignore the present. That is not healthy. These memories will always be fun to look back on years later when the pain is less severe and the memories begin to fade. These are the types of memories you always want to reinforce in your heart and mind, because we will never, nor do we want to, forget our children.

Sandy Fox's only daughter, Marcy, died in an automobile accident in 1994. Her new book, *Creating a New Normal . . . After the Death of a Child*, has more than 80 coping articles on surviving loss and many inspirational stories. Her first grief book is *I Have No Intention of Saying Goodbye*. Sandy has headed two national bereavement conferences for childless parents and speaks around the country. Read more of Sandy's articles at www.opentohope.com.

Valentine Poem from Dad to His Beloved Girl

By Alan Pedersen

One day in early February of 2007, I was driving near my home in Denver, listening to a local talk radio show. One of the hosts was setting up a commercial for a flower company he represented by saying that his young daughter was now at an age when he was going to send her flowers for Valentine's Day.

As he talked glowingly and lovingly of his daughter and his excitement about sending her a beautiful bouquet of all different-colored roses, it got me thinking about my Ashley. I began to imagine how wonderful it would be if I could send her roses on Valentine's Day, as well.

Ashley was my only daughter; she died in 2001 at the age of 18. The pain of not being able to shower her with gifts came flooding back to me. I had been in a writing slump, but when I went home that evening I kept thinking about roses and Ashley and Valentine's Day. I wrote this poem that I am happy to share with you.

A Dozen Roses
If I had a dozen roses, I know just what I'd do
I'd give each one a name that reminded me of you

The first rose I'd call sunshine, because you brighten every day
The second would be beauty, the kind that never goes away
The third rose would be priceless, like those hugs you gave to me
I'd name the fourth rose silly, oh how funny you could be
Rose five of course is patience, something you have helped me find
The sixth rose would be memories, the gift you left behind
The seventh and the eighth rose would for sure be faith and grace
Nine would be unique because no one can take your place
The tenth rose, well that's easy, I'd simply name it love
Eleven would be angel, I know you're watching from above
I'd think about that twelfth rose, and I'd really take my time
After all these roses are for you, my Valentine
I'm sending them to heaven in every color that I know
So twelve I'll name forever, that's how long
I'll love you so

Alan Pedersen's 18-year-old daughter, Ashley, was killed in an automobile accident in 2001. The tragedy led this award-winning singer/songwriter to write and record several CDs that share his message that grief and loss offer the opportunity for ordinary people to accomplish extraordinary things, and that healing begins when we give of ourselves. Alan plays his original music and speaks to grief organizations throughout the United States and Canada. He is the executive director of The Compassionate Friends/USA. Find more at www.opentohope.com.

Part 3:

Embracing Hope for Today and Tomorrow

Shadow of Grief
Still Lurks 20 Years Later

By Robert Thompson, MD

Although we know that after a loss the acute state of mourning will subside, we also know we remain inconsolable and will never find a substitute. No matter what may fill the gap, even if it is filled completely, it nevertheless remains something else. And actually this is how it should be. It is the only way of perpetuating that love which we do not want to relinquish.
—Sigmund Freud

This year marked a milestone regarding my son's death that I noted but did not celebrate. This was the year that Paul has been dead longer than he lived. To use an overused but nonetheless accurate word to describe my feelings, it felt "surreal." Thinking about it further, I realize that the whole experience of my son's death was surreal. From the moment of the first phone call through the funeral, memorial service, and the dark days that followed, it all had an unnatural feeling.

The first year's goal was to function, and somehow we did that. But after that first year, we had to learn to live and love and laugh again, and those are harder tasks. It's hard to laugh when the vulture of death is sitting on your shoulder and harder to love when acute pain wells up in you at unexpected moments.

Yet that is what we must do for our own sakes, the sakes of our partners, and truly for the good of everyone whose lives we touch. And most of all, we must do it for the child who has left us. And yet even now, we live in the shadow of our pain and awareness of our loss.

In a book first published in 1986, *Beyond Endurance: When a Child Dies*, Ronald J. Knapp describes six characteristics that parents who have suffered the loss of a child hold in common. His conclusions are not the result of theories formed in an academic vacuum, but rather research based on extended interviews with 155 families over a five-year period. In my opinion, it is still one of the most compassionate and best longitudinal studies of what parents experience after the death of a child, regardless of whether the death occurs suddenly and unexpectedly, or is the result of a prolonged illness or due to murder or suicide. One of the six characteristics is a term coined by Knapp, "shadow grief."

Shadow grief is a form of chronic grief. Knapp describes it as a painful awareness of the child's death that never goes completely away and that prevents us from fully experiencing the joys of living. While we function normally, shadow grief "is characterized by a dull ache in the background of one's feelings that remains fairly constant and . . . on certain occasions comes bubbling to the surface . . . always accompanied by a feeling of sadness . . . ."

By now, we have learned to choose those with whom we share stories of our child's life and perhaps the circumstances of his or her death. Such sharing on our part is not easily borne by everyone, so we pick and choose and sometimes move on to new friends. Our wish is not to burden others with our sadness. Yet the sadness engulfs us and affects who we are. Even if we are not defined by it, we are shaped by the grief and cannot run from it any more than we can run from our shadows.

Just as we can see our shadow better on some days than others, we are more aware of the shadow of our grief some days than others. On some days, it becomes very plain and bright, and at other times we say "good morning" to the grief and it recedes for the rest of the day. But the pain is always there, following us even if we and others can't see it. Shadow grief has become part of us and we of it.

Now, almost 20 years after my son's death, I embrace the shadow of my grief. Partly this is because it's there and I can no more deny it than I can deny my son's life, and partly because the pain serves to remind me of him and brings back memories that I find pleasant. I no longer care if others want to hear the story of my sorrow, and I don't feel any compulsion to share it unless there is genuine interest on their part. What once was important to me has become less so as I weave the tapestry of my own life. My son lives in my memory of him, and my grief shadow is his grief shadow, too. Grief over an uncompleted life snatched away in its prime.

Very recently, I was in the north woods just before sunrise, sitting on a stump and watching a brown creeper spiral down a large white pine tree. As the sun rose higher behind me, I watched my shadow lengthen on the ground. I thought about my son and the times we spent in the woods together, and the joys and humor that we shared with his brothers. Those memories, like my shadow, are always there and always comfort.

With apologies to the psalmist, "Yea, though I walk through the valley of the shadow of death" . . . I will live my life.

Dr. Robert R. Thompson's youngest son, Paul, was killed in a traffic accident in 1989 at the age of 18. After retiring from a long-acclaimed medical career in public service, Dr. Thompson decided he could help others who have lost children by describing the healing journey that he and his wife, Martha, took after Paul's death in his book, *Remembering: The Death of a Child*. The above article was previously published in *Living with Loss* magazine, "Living in the Shadow" by Robert R. Thompson, MD, Spring Issue, by Bereavement Publications, Inc., in the Healing the Body, Mind & Spirit Column, 2009. Read more by Robert at www.opentohope.com.

Seven Years Later, Still Coping with the Anniversary

By Kelly Farley

This past November marked the seven-year anniversary of losing my sweet daughter, Katie.

I'm not sure what happened to the last seven years, but they've managed to slip away. I know many of you are newly bereaved and probably think, "Seven years? I'm not sure if I can make one year or two years. How will I ever be able to make it to seven years?"

Those are excellent questions, questions I also asked myself at the beginning of this hell. I know the feeling of surviving second by second, and then moving to minute by minute, hour by hour, day by day, etc. Early in my grief, the thought of surviving a year seemed doubtful, but here I am, seven years later, writing an article about the horrific experience of losing a child. Obviously, it is still with me after all these years, but the pain of the anniversary days has faded.

I made a conscious decision at some point along the way that I was not going to run and hide from this day, because that's not possible. I knew I was going to find a way to celebrate Katie's life the best way I could. So the first year anniversary, my wife and I took the day off from work and spent the time reflecting on her life, what our life has become, and where we want our lives to go in a way to honor her.

Looking back over the last seven years, I have witnessed the transition from the person I used to be to the person I am today. I used to be pretty self-serving and intolerant of others, but I have now found a way to become a person who tries to serve others by helping them the best way I can.

Do I fail at this from time to time? Absolutely, but I would say this new direction in my life is one positive thing that has happened to me. Would I change it all to have her back? No doubt, but that's not an option I have, so I know I have to proceed with what I have control over and that's how I want to be known as a person.

The positive changes I've made in my life are a direct result of losing my sweet Katie. It is the gift of love, compassion, and understanding that Katie so graciously gave me.

I know there is a list of hundreds of negative things that have happened to us after the death of our children. Trust me, I have plenty. But what things have changed in your life that you would consider positive? If you can't think of anything positive that has happened in your life since the death of your child, what positives would you like to see happen in your life?

Kelly Farley is a bereaved father who experienced the loss of his two children over an 18-month span. He lost his daughter, Katie, in 2004 and his son, Noah, in 2006. During that time he realized there is a lack of support services available for grieving fathers. He is working on his first book as a resource for grieving dads, and he also created and maintains a website for this project. Read his articles at www.opentohope.com.

The Greatest Miracle
This Side of Heaven

By Chet Szuber

The last time I spoke to my 22-year-old daughter, Patti, I am sure I uttered the same words I'd said to her thousands of times before, "Have a good time, but be careful." Although Patti was the baby of the family, the youngest of our six children, she was selfless and a natural caregiver, expressing tender concern for me during my three heart surgeries and even pursuing a career in nursing. Patti loved the outdoors almost as much as she loved her friends and family, and she spent her final days on this earth surrounded by the majestic beauty of the Smoky Mountains, camping with a childhood friend.

Less than 12 hours after I spoke with Patti, my wife, Jean, and I were awakened by a predawn phone call. A doctor from the trauma center told us that Patti had been in a serious car accident. "Don't even bother coming down," the doctor said. "Her death appears to be moments away."

Jean and I were in Michigan, 700 miles from Patti. We were speechless, in shock, helpless. Our child, our baby, only 22 years old, was dying and there was nothing we could do. We couldn't even be with her. I don't know if anyone could ever accurately describe the emotions of a father at a time like this. The pain, confusion, and heartache are beyond description. As we sat in a stunned silence, I recalled a conversation that Patti had with us four years earlier about filling out an organ donor card. "Jean, you know Patti indicated a long time ago that if something like this happened, she wanted to be an organ donor. Should we let them know at the hospital?" She agreed, so I called the doctor back. "You do everything humanly possible to save this child," I told him. "But if things don't work out, it was Patti's wish to be an organ donor."

Nearly the whole family flew down to Knoxville to be with Patti. Her brain was dead, but doctors maintained life support to keep her organs viable and give the family time to say our farewells. My heart had broken anew after Patti's accident, but my heart had not been well for some time—I had congestive heart failure, and was on the heart transplant list. When we were just about ready to leave the hospital, the transplant coordinator came up to me and said, "We know you've been waiting for a heart for almost four years, Mr. Szuber. You can have Patti's heart."

In a state of shock and dismay, I turned down his offer immediately. I could not conceive of Patti's heart beating in my chest. Then, as I was walking to the hospital elevator, I heard Patti's voice, clear and vital. "Dad, take my heart," she said. "You've got to take my heart." While it may sound corny, I believe that Patti was pleading with me to accept her heart.

This would be the fourth surgery to open my chest, and there was a very real chance I would not survive the transplant. My family was very worried that I might die during the procedure. Waking up from the successful transplant was exhilarating and bittersweet. I knew my life would never be the same, and the last 12 years have been difficult at times, but I am grateful to be alive today because of Patti's gift.

When we got back to our farm in Michigan, Patti's many friends kept coming by the house. I began to find out, one by one, that many times Patti had said to each of them, "I wish there was some way I could give Dad my heart." My wife and I never knew Patti's wish until after the fact. If I had really stuck to my guns and refused Patti's heart and then discovered her wishes for me, I would have regretted that decision for the rest of my life.

I will never "get over" Patti's death. Life doesn't have a reverse button. We can't back up and change what has happened. I think I am able to cope a little bit better than most parents because Patti had helped so many people as an organ donor. Because of Patti's generosity, today two blind women have vision, two others share her kidneys, and another has her liver. She also donated about 30 bone and tissue samples, which helped victims of fire accidents and birth defects. Jean and I and her brothers and sisters know that Patti is gone, but she's not dead because she is alive in so many others. So that gives us a little comfort. I believe that I have experienced the greatest miracle this side of heaven.

Chet Szuber lives on a Christmas tree farm in Michigan, with his wife, Jean. He travels the world, speaking as an educator and advocate for organ donation and transplants. In his free time he enjoys hunting and golf. He has six children, including his daughter, Patti, who passed away at the age of 22, and is grandfather to 12 grandchildren. Listen to Chet's story at www.opentohope.com.

Being Available
for Turning Points

By Pamela Prime

After my son's death, there were many turning points along the way in my grief. I could not make them happen all by myself, but I could make myself available. At each turning point, there was a sense of Divine Grace; it was only in quiet reflection or in sharing the experience with a good listener that I could say "thank you."

I remember well the first time I could look at Sean's picture without breaking down in sobs. His suicide was shocking, terrifying, and beyond heartbreaking.

That memorable day, I sat on our sofa and looked at his face. Sweet, gentle tears rolled down my cheeks as I felt unbounded love flood my heart. I wrote in my journal, but it took a few days for me to name that extraordinary moment of grace and give thanks to God. The love I felt then still remains in my heart. It is what I have of Sean, and no one can take that from me!

Sitting on my closet floor one day, months after Sean's death, I slowly opened the suitcase in which I had saved some of his belongings. At that time, I did not recall what I had saved. I was in too much pain and confusion.

I held his clothes to my face, hoping to remember how Sean

smelled. I touched his poetry books, his baseball mitt, and his sunglasses with gentle caresses, hoping to recall how Sean felt. I folded up in tears on the closet floor with his things all around me and fell asleep.

I awakened, surprised by a sense of Sean's presence embracing me. I sat stunned by what had happened and felt so close to my son that I wondered if the veil had completely disappeared for a moment. Again, I wrote in my journal, but it was not until I shared this with my spiritual director that I wept in gratitude for that moment of pure grace.

There are many turning points on the journey of grieving the death of a loved one. Each is a reminder that we are not alone in our grief and that our loved ones are with us in spirit, as is our God. Our journeys are much greater than the healing of grief. They are awakening us to the presence of love in our midst and inviting us to participate in love, to become love itself, and to walk side by side with others who suffer with love in our hearts.

Pamela Prime's four-month-old daughter died of sudden infant death syndrome, and her son, at the age of 16, died of suicide. Pamela is a spiritual director, an educator, and a writer. Her first book is *When the Moon Is Dark We Can See the Stars*. Pamela is a mother and a grandmother and lives in California. To read more of her articles, visit www.opentohope. com.

Choosing Positive Memories

By Patrick T. Malone

We would have traded places with our child without a second thought, but we weren't given that choice. When that enormous pain of grief rolled into and totally disrupted our nice, neat, little life, we didn't have a choice. Even now, months or years later, when a residual wave of grief chooses to crash along our shoreline, we aren't given a choice. It just shows up.

None of us aspired to be part of TheCompassionate Friends. In fact, it ranks last in organizations that parents and families wish to join. We didn't choose this, but here we are.

So it is easy to allow this journey through our grief to make us its victim. Before long, I started treating every event in my life as if I didn't have a choice, and I became my worst nightmare. I became a victim.

Then, if we're lucky, something penetrates the fog of grief and depression and causes us to re-examine the manner in which we are working through our pain. For me, first, it was an article by my future friend, Rich Edler, which was published in *We Need Not Walk Alone* magazine. The specific line in the article was, "Grief is mandatory, misery is optional."

Second, it was the following poem by Howard Thurman, which appeared in a grief newsletter distributed by Dinah Taylor in Kentucky.

I Will Light Candles for Christmas

I will light candles this Christmas: Candles of joy despite all the sadness, Candles of hope where despair keeps watch, Candles of courage for fears ever present,
Candles of peace for tempest tossed days, Candles of grace to ease heavy burdens, Candles of love to inspire all my living, Candles that will burn all the year long.

The message is that we do have a choice. We cannot change the facts of what happened to our child, children, or grandchild. That is the past. We think we can plan for the future, but those plans may or may not have any effect on the actual future course of events. But we can do something about the here and now—the present.

So, when the next holiday season approaches and we prepare to light these candles in the memory of our children, let us choose, to the degree each of us is able, to create a positive memory of our child if only for the briefest of moments.

- Remember that vacation at the Magic Kingdom that she loved so much.

- Remember how he loved the Braves long before they started winning

- Remember that soccer match and how proud you were—not because he won, but because of the way he played.

- Remember how the dream came true when he made Drum Major of the band, but mostly remember he was part of finding the cure and that "ain't for nothing."

+ Remember how she loved Christmas and the light in her eyes whether she was giving or receiving.

+ Remember how much he loved to cook and the joy of making it his profession.

+ Remember her first day of school and how excited she was.

+ Remember all those scouting badges and how proud you were of all his efforts.

+ Remember how many of his college friends told you how much he had helped them.

+ Remember how hard she worked in school to make you a proud dad.

+ Remember his first smile, her first word, and their first steps.

+ Remember the warm days, bright sun, and flashing skis as she sailed effortlessly across the water.

+ Remember that slick, mischievous grin he flashed before he flipped down his visor and roared away on that purple motorcycle.

Some day, we will all see our children again, and when we do, they are going to ask what we did with the rest of our lives. I believe Scott, Erin, and Lance would be disappointed if I told them I spent the rest of my life grieving their deaths. That isn't how they want to be remembered.

However, I think they would be pleased if we are able to tell them that we lived the rest of our lives inspired by the positive memories of their lives.

So for the briefest of moments, set down your burden. Refresh yourself so that you can continue your grief journey buoyed by positive memories of a significant life, regardless of how long or short. A significant life lived well.

You have a choice. Choose well.

Patrick T. Malone's 25-year-old son, Lance, died in 1995 in a motorcycle accident. Earlier, his children, Scott and Erin, died as infants. Patrick is a senior partner with The PAR Group, with more than 35 years of experience in operations, customer service, and sales management. Patrick speaks extensively on the topic of surviving loss and has served in leadership positions and on the national board of The Compassionate Friends. Find his articles at www.opentohope. com.

I Chose to Live

By Louise Lagerman

Many bereaved parents think of ending their life after their beloved child dies. The pain cuts so deep and the longing to be with the child is so intense.

Four months after Keren died at age 23, I was so low, so empty, so depressed. I knew I couldn't live on this earth without her. I know, without a doubt, that my daughter broke through the realm of her dimension to save her mom. It was my daughter's gift to me.

I work as an in-home nurse to a sweet 90-year-old lady, who was napping at the time. The shutters were closed, her bedroom was very dark, and as I sat in the chair by the elderly lady's bed, I decided that on my way home that evening I would end my life to be with my daughter. I'd been thinking about it for weeks, but I had finally made up my mind at that moment. I was that lonely for my daughter.

Keren used to text me up to 20 times a day. Now my phone was silent, sad silence—just another reminder that my beloved daughter was gone and never coming home again.

I knew just how to kill myself. I had been thinking about it for weeks. To go home, I have to drive through Houston. On the highway, if I crashed my car through the barrier on this one ramp, I would fall six feet. Surely I would die and then I would be with my daughter again.

I felt such resolve about this. The beauty was that it would look like an accident, so I was hoping that would help spare my family a little. Even God wouldn't have been able to talk me out of it because, at that time, I was convinced there was no God. A loving God would not have taken my child.

As I contemplated this, my cell phone beeped. It was a text message. My phone had been so silent since my daughter died. Who could this be?

It was from my son, James, who was 17 at the time. The text read: "MOM I need you, I love you, please don't go. Stay here for me. I NEED you."

I was speechless. I was so shocked! James was a typical teen. His texts had always been simple: "Yes, Mom, I got to my friend's house safely. Stop bugging me."

How could he have known of my intention to crash my car?

My heart beating fast, my hands shaking, I dialed my son's cell phone. I said, "James, where are you?" He replied that he was at the mall with his girlfriend, who was trying on clothes.

"James, why did you text this to me?"

He said he had been sitting, just waiting for his girlfriend and, all of a sudden, he felt Keren strongly all around him. Keren said to him, "James, I want you to text this to Mom now!"

Keren was six years older than James and had always been very motherly toward him, and told him what to do a lot. So I have no doubt at all that it was my daughter trying to stop her mom from committing suicide, as I had planned. And she knew the one chance she had of stopping me was to have one of my sons connect with me at just the moment I needed to see and hear those words.

Since that day, I have not thought of joining Keren again

because I know that she wants me to stay here on Earth and be a mother to my two grown sons.

Louise Lagerman has worked in health care, specializing in the geriatric field, for many years. She recently founded Grief Support, a website for the bereaved. She is a mother to two sons, Eric and James, and her daughter, Keren, who died in 2006 at the age of 23. She lives with her husband, Steven, outside of Houston, Texas. Read more at www.opentohope. com.

Connecting to Nature:
Sacred Lessons Learned

By Dr. Jane A. Simington

I can hear Billy's voice saying, "Mom, can you come today? I want to show you the little river Wes and I found yesterday. It's full of minnows. It's in that marshy place where they cut down those old trees."

There were indeed minnows in his newfound stream. I returned, on numerous occasions, to ponder their existence. I returned to recall the precious moments my son, Billy, and I had shared. I returned to caress his foot's imprint in the muddy bog. I returned, praying that nature would preserve it—never taking it from me after he died suddenly and tragically at age 13.

One of the most difficult things to come to terms with was my need to know if Billy continued to exist in some spiritual form. The grief books, the counseling, and the support groups had each offered solutions to help manage the cognitive aspects of my grief, but for the anguish in my soul, they offered little reprieve.

I had read that the soul loves tranquility. My restless spirit longed for such a state. The masters said the answers lie within. Perhaps the key was in meditation. I tried various forms. I loved meditation and the breathing exercises that accompanied it.

I did not find the answers I sought. Instead I found silence, which I welcomed. It was a reprieve. I had not known silence for a long time. The nagging that had plagued my thoughts became less and less intrusive, and less and less demanding of my constant attention.

Ever so slowly, and ever so gently from within the place of silence, I came to know the peace of stillness. And in the stillness, I heard a whisper. I was being invited. There was no mistake. The voice was barely audible, but the message was clear. "Come to my meadow."

I accepted. I ran to the fields. The discovery was incredible. I ran. I walked. I loitered. I stayed. As the months went by, I delighted in the tender murmur that drifted on the breeze and floated with the raindrops. I was attentive to the whisper, and I heard it again and again and again, in the rustling of the willow branches, in the call of the coyote, and in the moan of the loon.

I lingered and was charmed by the whisper. I heard it in the laughter of the water as it rippled and tickled the rocks along its path in the gully. I was encouraged and attempted to laugh in unison.

I had not laughed in a very long time. Out in the prairie fields, far away from the eyes and ears of anyone who might think that I was on the verge of insanity, I forced myself to laugh. I did it again and again and again, day after day after day, until once again laughter was able to find its way out of my body of its own accord.

My path to the prairie field had become etched. I was gifted daily by the splendor and the lessons gained from the natural world. The field, the meadow, and the little river discovered by my son shared numerous tales of the continuing process of life. The lessons gained observing the natural order reinforced hope in the process of rebirth, and offered assurance that, somehow, somewhere, life continued even beyond death.

Why had it taken me so long to discover what was really valuable in life? I believe that Billy knew. In numerous ways throughout his young life, as well as since his death, he has guided me to view reality differently. While I would give anything to have learned the lessons his death taught me in less painful ways, I am aware that Billy has been my greatest teacher.

From my son, I have learned about priorities. He loved the natural world. I wish I had joined him more at the fishing holes and under the stars. There was much I could have learned. Had I been awake, I could have discovered, so much earlier, the sacred lessons available along the path.

Jane A. Simington, Ph.D., is the owner of Taking Flight International Corporation and the developer of both the Trauma Recovery Certification Program and the Grief Support Certification Program. She is the president of the Canadian Association of Trauma Recovery Providers, and frequently presents at conferences. An adjunct faculty member at several universities, she is the author of the book, *Journey to the Sacred: Mending a Fractured Soul*, from which the above article was excerpted. Her award-winning films include, *Listening to Soul Pain* and *Healing Soul Pain*. Read more at www.opentohope. com.

Despite Loss of My Son, It Remains a "Wonderful World"

By Laura Klouzek

I love the song "What a Wonderful World" by Louis Armstrong. I used to have it as a ringtone on my cell phone. I took it off my phone in 2008 when my son, Lucas, passed away. I heard it every time someone called during those two weeks to check on Lucas's progress or to see how we were faring as we lived in the waiting rooms at the hospital.

Lucas didn't get to come home with us when we left there. He had already left to be with his Father in Heaven. After that day, I had to take that song off my phone. I just didn't think it was such a wonderful world anymore.

I had always thought it was a pretty wonderful world.

God has always given me a hopeful, thankful outlook on life, and I have enjoyed more blessings than I can count. That ringtone just described how I felt most of the time. We had our share of hurts, trials, and struggles, but I could always look at my children and their families and find many blessings.

Then, in July of 2008, one of those wonderful blessings was ripped from us. Lucas was 33 years old and had been having some aches and pains. He had been in a minor car accident and believed his aches were just due to some injury that wouldn't quite go away. By June of that year, he was almost unable to work. Doctors couldn't find a problem. You don't usually look for cancer in a strapping 33-year-old man, who looked healthy and acted OK, except for the complaints of pain in his shoulders and then in his hip.

By the beginning of July, he had to rely on crutches and decided to see an orthopedic doctor since no one else could help him. The doctor ordered an MRI, took one look at it, and told Lucas he needed to see a different kind of doctor. We got him in to an oncologist within two days, and within two weeks he left us. He died from complications during surgery due to the cancer. My life would never be the same.

Lucas was my first child. He was also a husband and father. This was the child who made us laugh, then made us cry, and brought so much joy into our young marriage. I could picture his curly little head, and remember the tears I cried when he was born. And now God had decided Lucas should be with Him. No, it wasn't such a wonderful world. Even now, two years later, I break down in tears as I remember his life and his death. That is not the end of the story, though.

God has allowed me to cry, to scream at Him, to mourn, to remember. He has surrounded my husband and me with loving, supportive families. We still have our other children and their families, and we still get to see Lucas's wife, her new husband, and our grandchildren. Friends have walked alongside us, cried with us, and been there with a hug, a special word, or a card. I got to attend a grief support group with a special friend who had lost her husband. I have been able to walk with others who have had losses in their family.

Through our families, friends, and church, God has brought laughter back to our hearts. I believe we are more caring and compassionate due to our loss. Helen Keller once said, "What we have once enjoyed we can never lose. All that we love deeply becomes a part of us."

Yes, Lucas will always be a part of my heart and soul. I will always miss his love, his smart-aleck remarks, his smile. I will continue to cry, to sometimes be angry, to mourn, and to draw strength from others who have walked this same path. And I have changed the ringtone on my phone again. It goes, "And I think to myself, what a wonderful world."

Laura Klouzek's son, Lucas, died in July of 2008 after a short fight with cancer. His death and her journey through grief have prompted her to help others through her writing and speaking. Laura and her husband live in rural Missouri and are the parents of five children and the grandparents of eight, in addition to 12 years of life as foster parents. For more about Laura, visit www.opentohope.com.

About the Authors

Dr. Gloria Horsley and Dr. Heidi Horsley are a mother/daughter team of internationally recognized grief experts. They are the cofounders of the Open to Hope Foundation and cohosts of "Grief Relief" radio and "Grief Relief" television, an award-winning series. They cofounded the Open to Hope Foundation in memory of Scott, Gloria's son and Heidi's brother, who died in an automobile accident at age 17.

Dr. Gloria serves on the national advisory board for The Compassionate Friends and the Elisabeth Kübler-Ross Foundation. She writes a blog for Maria Shriver and *The Huffington Post*. Dr. Heidi is an adjunct professor at Columbia University and serves on the national board of directors for The Compassionate Friends, and on the advisory board for TAPS, the Tragedy Assistance Program for Survivors of Military Loss, and the Elisabeth Kübler-Ross Foundation.

Together Dr. Gloria and Dr. Heidi have written numerous articles and several books, including *Teen Grief Relief* and the award-winning *Real Men Do Cry*, which they coauthored with Eric Hipple. With the Open to Hope contributors, they have coauthored *Open to Hope: Inspirational Stories of Healing After Loss; Open to Hope: Inspirational Stories for Handing the Holidays After Loss; Fresh Grief: Inspirational Stories from OpenToHope. com; Spouse Loss: Inspirational Stories from OpenToHope. com;* and *Signs of Hope from Heaven: Inspirational Stories from OpenToHope.com.* Dr. Gloria also wrote *The In-Law Survival Guide.* Learn more at www.opentohope.com.

Dr. Gloria and Dr. Heidi are deeply indebted to the authors who graciously shared their journeys through grief in this book and the many more on the Open to Hope website.

Acknowledgments

As with our other books written with the Open to Hope contributors, a book like this comes together only through the dedication and selfless sharing of talent and energy from many, many people.

Thanks to each of our Open to Hope authors, who together have generously shared more than 3,000 wonderful stories and articles on www.opentohope.com. It was very challenging to select the stories to appear in this book. Thanks to Neil Chethik, our website's executive editor, and Heather Johnson, our Open to Hope Community Manager, for bringing these messages of care, healing, and hope together so seamlessly on our website.

Many thanks also to Beverly McManus and Karla Wheeler for their copy editing expertise and to Karla's team at Quality of Life Publishing for designing the cover and coordinating the publishing process. We so appreciate the support of our husbands and families, and of course, we are grateful for our loved ones who have gone before us and who inspired each of us to do this work and to share our stories.

—Dr. Gloria Horsley and Dr. Heidi Horsley

If you would like to apply to write about grief, loss,

hope and healing for the Open to Hope Foundation,

please go to www.opentohope.com and fill out the

section under "Write for Us."